Curtains, Blinds & Valances

Front cover (tl): Robert Harding Syndication/IPC Magazines (Dominic Blackmore);
(bl): Robert Harding Syndication/IPC Magazines (Polly Wreford);
(r): Robert Harding Syndication/IPC Magazines.

Page 3: Robert Harding Syndication/IPC Magazines; page 5: Eaglemoss/Paul Bricknell;
page 6: Eaglemoss/Mark Wood; page 7: Eaglemoss/Paul Bricknell;
page 8: Jane Churchill (tel:+44 171-493-2231).

First published in North America
in 1998 by Betterway Books
an imprint of F&W Publications Inc
1507 Dana Avenue
Cincinnati, Ohio 45207
1-800-289-0963

ISBN 1–55870–493–0

Manufactured in Spain

10 9 8 7 6 5 4 3 2 1

sew in a weekend

Curtains, Blinds & Valances

BETTERWAY BOOKS
Cincinnati, Ohio

Contents

1
Curtains and headings

Stitch up beautiful curtains in no time, then turn them into designer treatments with a variety of heading styles

2
Valances and pelmets

Turn ordinary windows into instant works of art with these unique ideas for curtain-top treatments

3
Blinds

Try these easy blind variations for an elegant yet
functional solution to difficult windows

4
Accessories

Dress up any window with these novel ideas
requiring little fabric and even less time

Index

Instant curtains

*You don't have to spend hours at the sewing machine
to make an impact at the window. A swathe of fabric
and some nifty clips could be all you need.*

Modern curtain design is all about simplicity and speed. It has a fresh, bright and breezy feel, far removed from traditional lined curtains and elaborately constructed drapery. It's also very flexible, so you can effect a lightning change to match the seasons, if you want – or even to match your mood!

There are lots of ideas around that are thoroughly lighthearted, and are guaranteed to inject a dash of fun into your room scheme. Choose a length of fabric and plunder the laundry basket for colourful plastic pegs to fix it at the window in a flash, for example; or cast a dreamy romantic haze over your bedroom with drifts of jewel-hued muslin, knotted over a pole and then allowed to drape down on to the floor.

To help you whiz up your new designs at the window, a whole range of clever products are available, such as no-sew heading tapes and clip-on curtain rings; for the curtains themselves, you can use virtually any textile item, even teatowels and table cloths.

Pegged up Cut a panel of fabric to fit the window pane and secure it with plain wooden household pegs, painted in bright, fruity colours. Clip the pegs on to a concealed length of wire, fixed to the window frame. The colourful mitred border frames the panel and is worth adding, if you have time.

Drape it

For curtains with confidence, fabric comes straight off the roll and goes up at the window, without even a glance at the sewing machine. Drape fabric casually over a pole and loop it into tiebacks to add real drama to a room. Or, make use of clever valance creators, drapery holders and rosettes in a variety of designs and materials – such as brass, iron or unobtrusive plastic.

Don't worry about the selvedges – you can lose them in the folds. Never mind the raw ends, as you can puddle the extra fabric on the floor and tuck the edge out of sight, or use one of the easy iron-on hemming tapes.

▶ *Tying the knot For draped effects, quantity and volume is everything, so it's better to buy an economical fabric and drape it lavishly, rather than skimp on a more pricey one. The knots in these curtains are hooked on to curtain holdbacks, to sweep the curtains into their elegant shape.*

◀ *Heavenly interiors This clever swag and tails treatment relies on three decorative holdbacks and lots of fabric. Use a few stitches to secure the fabric to the centre holdback and drape the rest of the fabric over the two outer ones. Sheer roller blinds provide further privacy.*

▼ *Clever clips Here is a selection of the clips you can buy. Some grip the fabric and then slip through ordinary curtain rings, and others have a built-in curtain ring. They are decorative, such as the shaped novelty clips, or plain and discreet.*

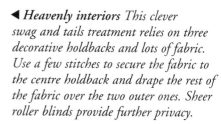

*Artistic influence
Many printed fabrics
are enhanced with a
mitred border to
frame them. Pick one
of the stronger colours
in the print to make
sure the border has
the desired impact.*

Border it

Firm fabrics with strong patterns are better shown off by displaying them almost flat, so that the power of the design is not lost in voluminous folds. A richly coloured, plain border, on all four sides, frames a good design and focuses attention like a picture frame, giving strength and body to the fabric edge as well. Make the border chunky – 5-7.5cm (2-3in) wide – for maximum effect, and select a plain fabric which echoes one of the main colours in the design. This is a clever way to make the most of an expensive fabric.

Clip it

The latest and easiest way to hang your curtains is with curtain clips. Whether you're hanging a delicate slip of sheer fabric, or a crunchily textured and neatly bordered panel, these clips make light work of the job, and add a charming detail as well. Available in brass, bronze and black iron effect, there are different types and styles to suit every situation.

HERE'S HOW

Skip the heading tape

For an informal window dressing that looks wonderful in a kitchen, hallway or bathroom, handstitch curtain rings directly on to the neatened top edge of the curtain. Multiply the width of the window by roughly one and half times, to give a little fullness, and use a ruler or tape measure to space the rings evenly – about 15cm (6in) is a good distance.

You will achieve the best results with lightweight fabrics, such as sheers, dressweight fabrics or light furnishing fabrics. For strength, use extra-strong polyester thread to secure the rings, rather than cotton thread.

Clever makeovers

Don't restrict yourself to just the furnishing fabric department when you're next looking for curtains. An imaginative eye will spy a window treatment in the most unexpected quarters. From classic linen glass cloths, colourful table cloths and fluffy travel rugs, through to embroidered throws and exotic saris, you can use practically anything – and if it comes ready finished at the edges, so much the better.

Accentuate any interesting edging detail by folding it over to make an attached valance – the fringing on a rug, for example, or the delicate filigree of lace on the edge of a table cloth. An old chenille sofa throw would make a sumptuous curtain to keep a room cosy from draughts; a glamorous silk scarf in dazzling colours could do duty as a blind, scooped up with ribbons.

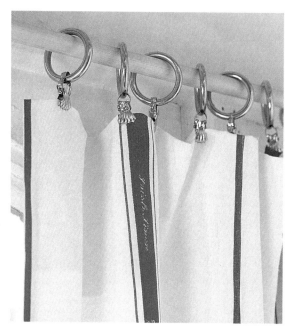

◀ Tea treats The humble tea towel, in best quality Irish linen, functions as a surprisingly smart curtain, held in place with decorative fan clips and gleaming curtain rings.

▼ Impromptu charm You can create a coordinated, fairly low cost look, by using items such as a bedspread or sofa throw to make impromptu curtains for a bedroom or living room. Just sew rings to the top edge, or fold one edge to make a self-valance and sew the rings along the crease.

▲ Lace tracery It's a shame to let beautiful lace table cloths languish in a linen chest or cupboard. Instead, display them in front of a window, where the delicate patterns are prettily enhanced by the light shining through. There is no need to damage the cloth with stitching, if you use curtain clips.

Making curtains 1

*The satisfaction of making your own window
treatment is enormous. You can achieve pleasing results
with a minimum of cost and time.*

Making your own curtains is surprisingly easy. You can speedily machine seams and hems, stitch on special heading tapes to produce pretty gathers or neat pleats, and add a truly professional touch with a sewn-in lining.

Getting started

Before you start making a pair of curtains, you need to measure up the window to calculate the size of each curtain and the quantity of fabric (and lining) required. You also need to decide on:

◆ A suitable fabric for your chosen window treatment – unlined or lined, formal or casual.
◆ The type of heading tape and suitable curtain hooks.
◆ The method of hanging the curtains, either by track or by pole, and the position of the track or pole.
◆ The length of the curtains – sill, floor or in between.

Choosing fabrics

You can use a huge variety of fabrics for making lined or unlined curtains. To make life easier for yourself, choose a plain fabric or one with an all-over pattern like sprigs or stripes to avoid the need for pattern matching.

Unlined curtains Sheers, such as filmy voile or muslin, crisp light cotton prints or weaves and cotton/polyester blends and heavy, draught-proofing tapestries are all suitable.

Lined curtains Some fabrics, such as furnishing cotton, chintz, linen or textured weave, look better made up as formal curtains with a lining to add fullness and elegance.

◀ *A pair of elegantly draped full-length curtains looks smart at a French window. A lining adds weight and fullness to the curtains.*

Heading tapes

Most curtains are made with a certain amount of fullness in the width, which means that the total fabric in a pair of curtains is a good deal wider than the width of the window. The fullness is gathered in at the top of each curtain by the pull-cords in a heading tape.

Ready-made heading tapes are available in a number of different styles to suit various decorating looks. Pencil pleat and standard heading tapes are good for a simple gathered look.

You need to know which tape you are going to use before you buy your fabric, because each type of heading tape gathers up the fabric by different amounts (its gathering allowance). Generally, you need to allow for fabric that is at least twice the width of the finished curtain to achieve the necessary fullness.

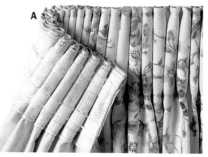

▲ *Pencil pleat tape* (**A**) *and* *standard* *tape* (**B**) *create neatly gathered curtains.*

▶ *Standard curtain hooks* *are used for* *hanging simply pleated curtains. The* *hooks slot into pockets in the heading tape* *and through screweyes in the curtain rings* *or track gliders. They are made in brass* *for carrying heavy curtains and white* *plastic for medium to lightweight curtains.*

Tracks and poles

If you do not already have a track or pole fixed above the window, you can find a wide selection in most department and hardware stores. When choosing a new one, make sure you pick the right weight for the curtains you are going to make – lightweight for sheers or unlined cotton fabrics, mediumweight for sill-length curtains and heavyweight for lined, floor-length curtains.

Curtain poles have curtain rings threaded along their length and curtain hooks are slipped through a small screweye in each ring. For a period look, you can choose a wood-stained or antiqued-brass pole, or for a more contemporary feel a painted wooden or black-iron pole.

What length of track or pole?

When measuring up for a new track or pole, remember to allow extra on either side of the window so that you can draw the curtains well back. An allowance of 10-20cm (4-8in) on each side is customary, depending on the width of the curtains and the thickness of the fabric. If you want to make the window appear wider, you can increase the allowance slightly on either side.

Fixing a track or pole

Take a good look at your window and work out the best height to fit the new track or pole. As a guide, fix the track or pole between 7.5-12.5cm (3-5in) above the window. If there is only a small space between the ceiling and the top of the window, a track is a better solution than a pole, as a pole plus rings is a tight squeeze and the curtain may drop below the top of the window.

Whether you choose a track or a pole, it must be securely fixed to the wall. Use the brackets supplied and follow the manufacturer's instructions.

Decorative tracks have a simple design printed along the front which is on show when the curtains are drawn back.

Curtain tracks are strips of plastic or metal fitted with runners which slide freely along them. Each runner has an eye or loop at its base, through which you slot a curtain hook that is held in the heading tape.

Corded tracks have a set of pull-cords attached. Draw the curtains using the pull cords to prevent damaging or dirtying the curtain fabric.

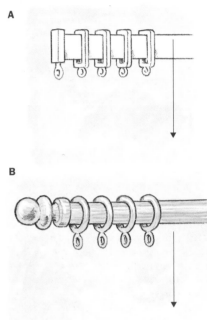

◄ *Just-below-sill length curtains in a fresh daisy print emphasize the neatness of a small window. Letting them hang freely from a simple pole enhances the informal feel.*

Measuring the length

Once you have chosen the appropriate length for your curtains, taking accurate measurements of your window with a retractable metal rule is the first step to making successful curtains. Whenever possible fix the new track or pole in position above the window before measuring.

A

B

Measure from the top of the track (**A**) or the screweye at the bottom of the ring (**B**) to the required finished length. To work out the length of fabric you need to cut, add 20cm (8in) for the heading and hem allowances. Then for sill-length or floor-length curtains deduct 1cm (⅜in) to make sure they hang just above the windowsill or floor.

Measuring the width

Measure the width of the track or pole (**E** in the diagram in the box on the left). This is the finished width of the curtains. Divide the full width by the number of curtains you are hanging to determine the finished, gathered width of each curtain.

With an overlap track, where the curtains pull one in front of the other rather than simply meet in the middle, measure the length of the overlap arm and add the extra width to one curtain.

Which length?

When you are deciding on the length of the curtains you want for a window, the style and function of the room have as much bearing as the size of the window itself.

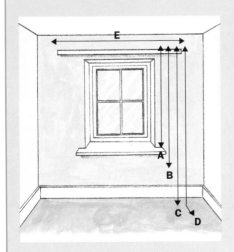

Sill-length (**A**) curtains are practical in kitchens, bathrooms and children's bedrooms, or for tiny cottage-style and dormer windows. The curtains should be 1cm (⅜in) above the sill so that they sweep clear of it.

Between sill and floor (**B**) is a second option, but it can look half-finished if the proportions are not right for the window. Check the effect by draping some spare fabric or an old sheet to the length you want.

Floor-length (**C**) curtains add elegance and insulation to living and dining rooms, master and guest bedrooms. For an exaggerated designer effect, you can add a little extra to the full length (**D**) so that the curtains drape or puddle slightly on the floor.

Calculating fabric amounts

For a small window you may need only one width of fabric for each curtain drape. For larger windows you may have to sew a couple of fabric widths together for each drape.

To work out how many widths you need, first decide which type of heading tape you are using. Most tapes, including standard and pencil pleat, require a double fullness – the fabric should be twice the width of the track. Multiply the track width by two, divide this amount by the width of the fabric –120-140cm (48-54in) is usual. Round up to the nearest full width.

Multiply the cut length by the number of widths required.

The chart below gives a working example of how to calculate the amount of fabric you will need for making curtains. There is also a blank column for you to fill in the measurements of your own window and fabric requirements.

▶ *Floor-length curtains and a coordinating blind are a practical and elegant partnership.*

	Example		Your window	
Curtain length	cm	in	cm	in
Finished length of each curtain	200	80	—	—
+ Hem/heading allowance (for 7.5cm (3in) hem)	20	8	20	8
Total cut length	220	88	—	—
Curtain width	cm	in	cm	in
Width of pole or track	170	68	—	—
x Allowance for gathering	2			—
Total width for each curtain (add track overlap allowance here)	340	136	—	—
÷ Fabric width	122	48	—	—
Total number of fabric widths needed		3		—
(For a pair of curtains, 1½ widths per curtain)				
Total fabric needed	cm	in	cm	in
Total cut length	220	88	—	—
x Total number of widths		3		—
= **Total fabric length**	660	264	—	—
SO BUY:	6.6m	7 ½yd	—	—
			—	—

Pattern repeats

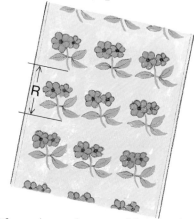

If you have chosen a fabric with an obvious repetitive design motif, you need to make sure the motifs line up across each curtain and at the seams, as well as from curtain to curtain. To ensure that you will be able to do this you generally need to buy extra fabric.

To work out how much extra fabric you need, you have to know the depth of the pattern repeat (**R**). Ask the sales assistant for the pattern repeat or measure it yourself, taking the vertical distance from the top of one motif to the top of the next identical one.

When you are calculating how much fabric to buy, add the pattern repeat on to the total cut length and multiply by the number of widths as usual.

Making curtains 2

Simple curtains, with a heading tape to gather them, are easy to make and suit most windows. Find out how to sew them either with or without a lining.

When you are making curtains to dress a window, you have the choice of leaving them unlined for a light, informal effect or adding a lining to gain weight and elegance. Your decision depends largely on the location of the window and the style of the room.

If privacy and insulation are not a priority, a pair of almost see-through unlined curtains made in textured cotton, cool linen or ritzy taffeta is a good way to screen a window and filter a mellow light into the room. Unlined cotton curtains are also a practical window treatment for a kitchen or bathroom, because you can wash and dry them in a few hours.

Adding a lining to your curtains has several benefits. Primarily, it makes the curtains look fuller and improves their hang. A lining also helps to keep out draughts, reduce heat loss and protect the fabric from dust and sunshine.

▲ *A floor-length unlined curtain, in a sunny yellow cotton print, screens the window for privacy yet still allows light to filter into the room. It is surprisingly easy to make curtains and achieve professional looking results, when you use one of the special heading tapes designed for the purpose.*

Working with patterned fabrics

When you are making curtains from a fabric with a directional design, they look much smarter if you can arrange whole motifs along the hemline and match the pattern between joined widths.

Positioning the pattern

1 Cutting first width
Decide on the best position for the lower edge of the curtain once it is hemmed in relation to the pattern motifs and mark this with a pin on each selvedge. Then cut the bottom raw edge 15cm (6in) below this line. Measure the cut length up from this edge, mark and cut.

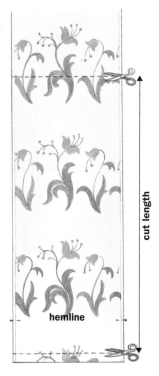

second width

first width

hemline

cut length

2 Cutting further widths
Move up to exactly the same point in the pattern as the bottom raw edge of the first width and cut across in a straight line. The lower edge of the next width is then at the correct point in the pattern. Measure, mark and cut as before until all widths are cut.

Joining widths

If you are working with an uneven number of fabric widths for your curtains, divide one width in half lengthways and join one half on to the outer edge of each curtain, matching selvedges so that the seams are less noticeable.

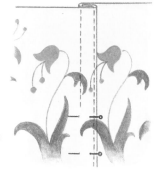

▲ When you are hanging a pair of curtains, one on either side of a window, it is important that the pattern matches across the two curtains for the most pleasing results.

1 Matching the pattern
Press the seam allowance under along one side and lay the folded seam on top of the adjoining width with the pattern matched. Pin in place. Working from the right side and using matching thread, pin and stitch close to the folded edge through all layers.

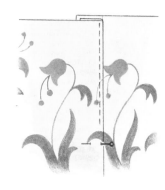

2 Neatening the seam
Turn to the wrong side and trim the lower seam allowance to 6mm (¼in). Fold the wider seam allowance in half over the narrower one, enclosing it, and press. From the right side, pin and stitch down the seam again, 6mm (¼in) from first stitching line, catching turnings at back.

Unlined curtains

You need a wide, clear and flat surface to lay out the fabric for cutting out and pinning widths together. A clean floor is ideal, unless you have a large work surface.

1 Measuring up Following the instructions given in *Making curtains 1*, measure the window and work out the amount of fabric required.

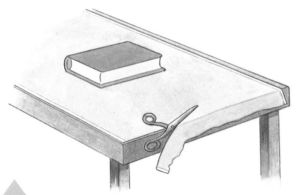

2 Straightening the ends Iron out creases in the fabric. To straighten the fabric end, line up the selvedge with the edge of a table, using the corner to get a right angle, and trim the fabric.

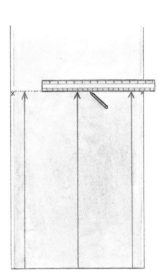

3 Cutting the lengths With the fabric wrong side up, measure the cut length from the trimmed straight edge and use tailor's chalk to mark it on both selvedges and in the centre. Cut the first width to length along the marked line. Repeat for all remaining widths. If you are using an odd number of widths, fold the last width in half lengthways and cut along the fold. To match patterns across the widths and join half widths, refer to the steps on the page opposite.

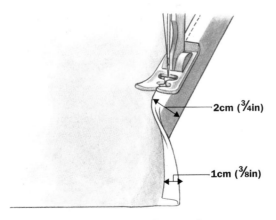

4 Stitching the side edges Turn under 1cm (³⁄₈in) then 2cm (³⁄₄in) to the wrong side down each side of the curtain. Press and stitch close to the inner fold.

You will need

- ◆ Curtain fabric
- ◆ Scissors
- ◆ Metre rule (yardstick)
- ◆ Tape measure
- ◆ Pins
- ◆ Dressmaker's pencil or tailor's chalk
- ◆ Standard or pencil pleat curtain heading tape
- ◆ Matching thread
- ◆ Curtain track and curtain hooks
- ◆ 2 Cord tidies (optional)

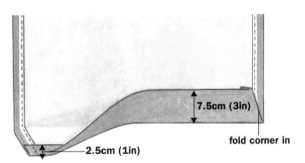

5 Turning up the hem Turn under 2.5cm (1in) then 7.5cm (3in) along the bottom edge and press. Fold the corners of the hem in at an angle at each end until they align with the side hems.

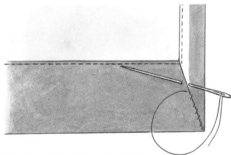

6 Stitching the hem Machine stitch along the hem close to the fold, right up to the side hem. To finish, slipstitch neatly down the folded corners.

Tip

COPING WITH SELVEDGES

On some fabrics, the selvedge is often more tightly woven than the rest of the fabric, which can result in puckered seams that spoil the hang of the curtains. To prevent puckering, snip into the selvedges at 10cm (4in) intervals.

length to eye of runner/ring + 1cm (³⁄₈in)

8 Positioning the tape Cut a length of heading tape, the width of the curtain plus a 2.5cm (1in) overlap at either end. On the wrong side, centre and pin the heading tape along the top of the curtain, 1cm (³⁄₈in) from the fold. Pin along the lower edge of the tape too, trimming the edge of the fabric if necessary so that it is covered by the tape.

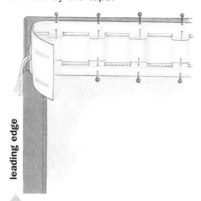

leading edge

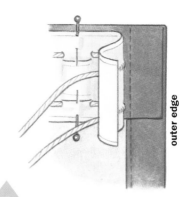

outer edge

10 Neatening the outer tape edge Pull out the cords on the right side of the tape and leave them free. Turn under 2.5cm (1in) of tape.

11 Stitching the tape To prevent puckering, stitch along the top and bottom edges of the heading tape in the same direction. Then, leaving the two cords free at the outer edge, stitch across the ends of the tape.

7 Preparing the heading On the right side measure the required length of the curtain from the bottom edge, add 1cm (³⁄₈in) and mark with pins at intervals across the width of the curtain. Fold the remaining fabric over to the wrong side and press.

9 Neatening the inner end of tape At the leading edge, where the curtains meet at the centre, pull out the tape cords from the wrong side of the tape and knot them together securely. Turn under 2.5cm (1in) at the end of the tape, covering the knotted cords.

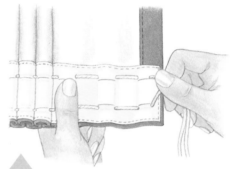

12 Gathering the curtains Pull up the loose cord ends evenly until the curtain is gathered to the right width. Make a knot in the cords near the heading tape to hold the gathers. Wind the surplus cords round a cord tidy or into a neat bundle. Slip the cord tidy into the heading tape or catch the wound cord with two stitches to the top of the curtain.

13 Inserting curtain hooks Adjust the gathers evenly across the curtain. Insert a curtain hook into the end pockets of the curtain tape. Fold the curtain in half and insert a hook at the centre. Space out the other hooks every 10cm (4in) in between. Check that there is a track runner or curtain ring for each hook in the heading tape and hang the curtains.

◀ *The fresh blue and yellow print used to make these drapes is so strong and eye-catching in its own right that it doesn't need complicated styling. Using a standard pencil pleat heading and hanging the curtains from a simple timber pole is dressing enough.*

Simple lined curtains

1 Cutting out and joining widths Cut the same width and length in lining as curtain fabric, following *steps* **1-3** for *Unlined curtains*. If necessary, join the widths and press the seams open.

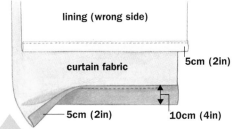

lining (wrong side)

curtain fabric

5cm (2in)

5cm (2in)

10cm (4in)

2 Turning up the hems For the curtain, turn under 5cm (2in) and then 10cm (4in) on the bottom edge of the fabric, press and stitch close to the fold, leaving 15cm (6in) at each end unstitched. For the lining, turn up a double 5cm (2in) hem, press and stitch close to the fold across the entire width.

3 Preparing the fabric and lining Right side up, lay the hemmed curtain on the work surface. Centre the hemmed lining, right side down, on top, matching any seams and setting the base of the lining 4cm (1½in) above the bottom of the curtain.

◀ *Full-length curtains can be cut to puddle slightly on to the floor. For a graceful line, sweep the curtains away from the window with tiebacks.*

▼ *Gathered up tightly, a standard pencil pleat heading forms a row of regular concertina pleats.*

In this straightforward method of lining curtains, the curtain and lining are machine-stitched together down each side and treated as one when adding the top heading but separately at the hems. To ensure that lined curtains hang well, allow 15cm (6in) for a more substantial double hem instead of the 10cm (4in) allowance for unlined curtains. In addition to the materials for making unlined curtains, you need as much lining as curtain fabric.

Lining fabrics

Standard curtain lining, a cotton sateen usually in beige, cream or white, is generally not washable, although you can wash polyester lining in a washing machine. Coloured linings enhance the curtain fabric and increase the variety of colours in a room.

Lining fabrics come in two standard widths – 122cm (48in) and 138cm (54in) – so that you can pick the width that's closest to your fabric width. You need to buy the same amount of lining as the fabric. If the fabric is much wider than the lining, you have to buy an extra width of lining.

Blackout lining has a rubbery finish on the wrong side and is good at cutting out light in bedrooms. It isn't washable. **Aluminium-coated lining** is an effective insulator. Although expensive, you recover its initial cost by saving on heat loss in the winter. During the summer, it reflects back the sun's rays to keep the room cool.

4 **Joining the lining to the fabric** Use a metre rule (yardstick) to smooth out any wrinkles in the two layers. Then trim the sides of the lining so that it is 6cm (2¼in) narrower at each side than the fabric. Bring the edges of the lining and fabric together and pin. Stitch from the top, taking a 1.5cm (⅝in) seam allowance, stopping 5cm (2in) above the fabric hem.

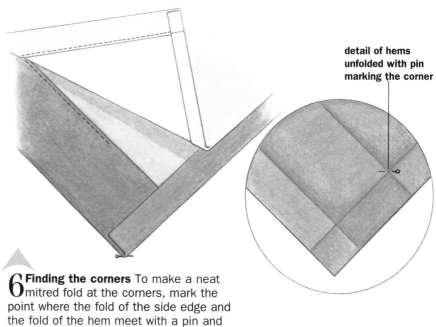

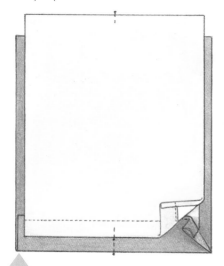

6 **Finding the corners** To make a neat mitred fold at the corners, mark the point where the fold of the side edge and the fold of the hem meet with a pin and open out the fabric.

detail of hems unfolded with pin marking the corner

5 **Turning out to the right side** Turn the curtain out to the right side, matching and pinning any seams. If there are no seams, mark and match the centre of both the fabric and the lining. Smooth out to the side with the metre rule, so that the fabric wraps to the wrong side to form a 3cm (1¼in) hem on the side edges. Press the side edges.

7 **Folding the corners** Fold the fabric diagonally across the corner so that the pin is exactly on the edge of the fold and the top and side of the flap are parallel to the bottom and side of the curtain.

▼ *Short curtains are often the best choice for a small window, especially in an informal situation.*

8 **Re-folding the hems** Crease along the fold and then turn in the side hem, followed by the base hem. Slipstitch the edges of the mitre together and along the unstitched part of the hem. Pull the lining down over the fabric hem and slipstitch down each side and along the bottom edge for 2.5cm (1in).

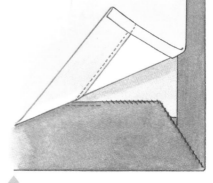

9 **Finishing the curtain** Continue with *steps* **7-13** for *Unlined curtains*, treating the lining and fabric as one layer when attaching the heading tape.

Lace and sheer curtaining fabrics

*Dressing your windows with lace or sheer fabrics is a
simple affair. The only difficulty is choosing from the wide
range of exquisite fabrics on offer.*

*Team crisp white
lace curtains with
a fresh red and
white gingham
valance for a bright
country look.*

The range of sheer furnishing fabrics is constantly changing to cope with new fashions and the increasing popularity of the sheer look. As well as traditional lace and net curtaining, shops now offer a tempting array of plain and printed voiles and muslins. Fibre content also varies widely, from polyester and nylon to natural cotton and linen, with many easy-care mixtures too.

Lace or net curtains provide a degree of privacy and filter out strong sunlight. The new voiles and muslins perform the same functions, but give a more streamlined look, suitable for the modern home. Printed voiles introduce pattern into a room – stars, suns and cherubs are popular designs.

For purely visual appeal, use sheer curtains on their own; a fabric valance adds extra interest, while an opaque roller blind gives night-time privacy. Or, for a more dramatic effect, give a bedroom a romantic makeover by hanging sheer drapes from a four-poster or coronet, or casually drape them over a pole. You can also use lace and sheers to make Austrian, London, Roman and roller blinds, although you must stiffen the fabric first for a roller blind.

Buying sheer curtaining

What makes buying sheer curtaining fabric different from other soft furnishing fabrics is that, in addition to being sold on the roll, it is also available almost ready-to-hang. Fabrics with prepared slot headings and hems are available in different drops (lengths). All you have to do is to select the appropriate drop, buy enough to cover the width of your window, then simply hem the side edges. Nets and lace woven with specially neatened selvedges are another good option, as they replace the need to neaten the side hem edges of the curtain.

Types of sheer furnishing fabrics

Café curtain lace is sold in drop lengths of 30-80cm (12-31½in). The lower edge is usually shaped or frilled, and the top edge is finished with either a casing or eyelets. It is available in cotton, polyester or cotton/polyester blends.

Lace and net curtaining is available in a variety of widths and drops, often with a pre-finished top and hem edge to eliminate the need to join widths. The hem edge may be finished with a hem, frill or neatened border and the top edge with a pre-stitched casing. These short nets come in a range of drop lengths, from 100-228cm (40-90in). For long windows, buy fabric with neatened selvedge edges; they come in varying widths – from 150-300cm (60-118in).

Lace curtaining is available in cotton, polyester and cotton/polyester blends. Cotton lace has a matt finish and is slightly heavier in weight than polyester.

Lace panels are ready-made rectangular panels of lace with a finished border around all edges. Designed to hang flat or slightly gathered, they come in various sizes for hanging at medium-large windows and in front of glass doors.

Muslin is a semi-sheer, translucent fabric, usually made from 100 per cent cotton. It is available in white, cream, dyed and printed and comes in several widths, from 130cm (50in) to 300cm (118in).

Valance lace is available to coordinate with full length lace curtaining. It is sold in valance length drops – about 30cm (12in) – and you buy it by the metre or yard. To make a gathered valance, stitch gathering tape to the top edge and then hang the finished valance from a special valance track. Some designs feature a frilled hem edge, or a shaped hem edge that curves down at the sides. It is available in cotton, polyester or cotton/polyester blends.

Voile is a sheer fabric, usually made from 100 per cent cotton. It is widely available in plain white and cream, and white and cream printed with designs. Linen voile is also available and has a coarser, crunchier appearance. A more recent innovation is coloured voile for sheer curtains, and voile printed with all-over coloured designs – such as floral patterns and checks. Like muslin, it is available in a range of widths.

Fabric care

Pre-shrinking
Most lace and net fabrics shrink by about 10 per cent when you wash them, so pre-shrink the fabric by washing it before making up the curtains.

Laundering
Unless machine washing is indicated on the fabric label, wash all sheer curtaining by hand. Soak first in lukewarm soapy water, using a biological detergent to retain a dazzling white colour, if necessary. Special net whiteners are also available. Allow the fabric to dry naturally in an airy place, away from direct sunlight. Stretch it gently, while still slightly damp to regain original width and length.

Pressing
Synthetic fabrics Avoid pressing – hang them up while they are still damp so the creases fall out.
Cottons Press with a cool iron.

dyed muslin

printed muslin

polyester v

dotted voile

cotton lace panels

colour-woven checked muslin

printed mu

Stitching tips

Making lace and sheer fabrics into drapes is quite easy. If you have bought a fabric with a pre-made casing and hem, all you need to do is hem the sides. If the fabric has neatened or bordered side edges, you need only hem it and add a casing or heading tape to the top edge.

If your fabric does not have a pre-made casing and hem, you must straighten the edge of the fabric before cutting each length. To do this, simply draw out two or three threads across the width and cut straight across the line that is left.

Seams

Buy the correct width of fabric for your window or bed drapes, so that you do not need to stitch a seam. If you have to use more than one width, you can hang the widths side by side without seaming. If, for some reason, you feel that you do need to stitch a seam or join widths together – if the selvedges are a little rough, perhaps – use a flat fell seam.

For sheer fabrics, use a fine polyester or transparent thread. Set the stitch length to a slightly shorter stitch than usual and always stitch a sample first to check the tension – some sheer fabrics wrinkle when stitched. For stitching nets, use a long, narrow zigzag in place of straight stitch, and for lace, use a long, wide zigzag.

Needles and stitches

- ◆ **Machine needles** Sizes 70/9 or 80/11
- ◆ **Stitch length** 1.5-2 millimetres (20-15 per inch)
- ◆ **Hand needles** Betweens sizes 9 to 11
- ◆ **Thread** Fine polyester, cotton-wrapped polyester, or transparent

▶ *Two layers of semi-sheer muslin, secured with simple tie fastenings, reveal just how easy it is to add colour to an otherwise plain interior. Wooden shutters serve to provide privacy and keep out the light, when necessary.*

Hems

When you are hemming polyester, or polyester-blend net and lace curtains, measure, pin and tack the hems in place first. If you need to press the hem, adjust the iron to the coolest setting and press it after stitching.

Side hems Turn under a double 1.2cm (½in) hem down each side edge of the lace curtain. Pin, tack and stitch the hem close to the inner folded edge.

Base hem Turn a double 6cm (2¼in) hem along the base edge of the lace curtain. Pin, tack and stitch the hem close to the inner folded edge.

Deeper hems Hems up to double 15cm (6in) deep look elegant on longer windows. Make sure that the bottom edge is perfectly straight before hemming, though, as any imperfections will be clearly visible.

Hanging drapes

There are many ways of hanging sheer drapes – conventionally with a casing or eyelets, or you can use a gathered heading tape with a track or pole. A stylish, up-to-date look is achieved by using fabric clips attached to a pole.

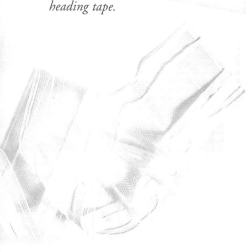

Ready-made casings take the hard work out of making sheer curtains. You can also buy a special translucent heading tape for sheers (see below). Simply stitch it along the curtain top in the same way as a normal heading tape.

Making a casing

The traditional method for hanging sheer curtains is from an elasticated wire or slim plastic or brass rod. To hang the fabric, stitch a casing along the top edge, either with or without a stand-up frill.

▲ *Delicate daisies and scalloped edging on the sides and hem give the perfect finish to this fine net panel. A simple casing secures it on a fine brass rod.*

Casing without a frill
Turn under a double hem about 3cm (1¼in) deep. Stitch close to the inner folded edge, and again close to the top folded edge.

Casing with stand-up frill
Add 3cm (1¼in) to the casing depth for the stand-up frill. Turn under a double hem of 6cm (2¼in) for a 3cm (1¼in) casing. Stitch close to the inner folded edge, and again 3cm (1¼in) above the first row of stitching.

Hanging sheer curtains

Making and fitting your own lace or sheer curtains
couldn't be simpler – much of the work is already done
for you, and the effects can be truly magical.

With all the delightful new ranges of sheer fabrics in the shops, you can transform the appearance of a window in record time – the curtains are so light they don't need heavy fittings and brackets and there's a wide choice of easy ways to hang them.

Whether you want to screen a window for privacy, or just pretty it up by framing it with delicate translucent folds of sheer or lace fabric, there is a fitting or rod just perfect for the job. Some curtain rods need no fitting at all – a hidden spring keeps it snugly in place.

There are all sorts of specially made heading tapes for window treatments that you can look out for. However, the easiest way to hang sheer curtains is with a cased heading, through which the rod or wire is simply slotted.

▲ *A simple cased heading maintains the light and airy look of this delicate voile fabric and shows off the unusual silvered finials of the rod. Privacy is provided by the blind which hangs behind the sheer drapes.*

Heading tapes and fixing methods

Start by selecting a heading tape that suits the weight of the fabric and the proportion of the curtains. Then choose from a range of rods, tracks, clips and poles and other fittings specially suited to hanging decorative sheer fabrics.

Lightweight tracks (A) of either plastic or aluminium are slim and unobtrusive. They are a practical choice, as you can pull the curtains across the window or open them to let the breeze in. Flexible plastic tracks can be bent around bays.

Narrow gathered tape (B) is ideal for very delicate fabrics and makes a dainty heading on short curtains.

Plastic-covered wire (C) is the simplest way to hang lightweight curtains in a recess or directly on to the window frame. It is a stretchy spiral of wire sheathed in plastic and comes in ready-cut rolled lengths – just choose the next size up to your required length. For fixing wires, see the steps, below right.

Press 'n' drape (D) is a special heading tape with a fuzzy backing which clings to the hard side of Touch and Close tape. The tape is stitched to the top of the curtain in the usual way and gathered up. The hard side of the tape is stuck or stapled to the window frame or wall above the window. The curtain is then simply pressed in place.

Rods and poles (E) There is a wide range of narrow poles and rods which are useful for hanging fine curtains. Look for period-style, brass café rods with tiny brass finials, or recess brackets to fit into a recess. Small plastic-covered rods are also suitable and have the advantage of being easy to wipe clean. Alternatively, use any of the rods and poles sold for standard curtains.

Smocked and other novelty tapes (F) make a lovely feature on sheer curtains and work well as they are not too bulky.

Telescopic tension rods (G) have a spring concealed inside them. You compress the ends to slide the rod into position in a window recess or frame. When it is released, the rod is tensioned firmly in place by the spring. Buy the size range to suit your width of window.

Telescopic tension rods are used with a cased headed curtain – push the rod through the casing before fitting into place. Or try special curtain (crocodile) clips, which slip over the rod and grip the curtain with tiny teeth – doing away with the need for hooks completely.

Transparent tape (H) eliminates the chance of an ugly shadow forming behind a sheer or fine fabric. Use clear plastic hooks with this tape, or whenever you are using sheer or fine fabrics.

▼ *A filmy lace panel, hung from a plastic-covered wire slotted through a plain hem, gently filters light in a bathroom while giving some privacy.*

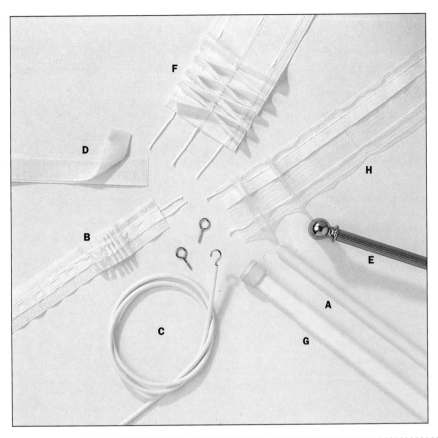

Deciding on fullness

The type of fabric you choose and the style you are aiming for determines how much fullness you put into your curtains. Crunchy textured lace is best left quite loosely gathered, or in flat panels, to allow the light to cast shadow patterns through it; fine voiles look wonderful swirling across the window in rich folds. To help you decide, use the chart below to determine the correct fullness for the job. But remember that this is only given as a guide, and the way you use the fabric depends on the look you want to achieve.

Curtain Fabric	Gathering Allowance
Lace panels	width times 0
Heavy lace	width times $1\frac{1}{2}$
Decorative semi-sheers	width times $1\frac{1}{2}$
Voiles	width times 2
Fine nets	width times 2
Very fine voiles	width times 3

Fixing plastic-covered wire

The most cost effective way of hanging sheers is to use plastic-covered wire. It's easy to fix, but must be taut to prevent it from sagging. Over wide windows, add a central cup hook.

You will need

- Length of plastic-covered wire
- Two screw eyes
- Two screw-in hooks
- Pencil
- Bradawl
- Pliers

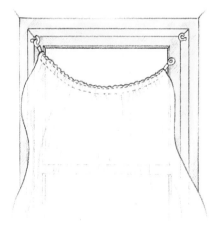

3 **Hanging the curtain** Screw in the remaining eye in the end of the wire; push this end through the casing of the curtain, stretch the wire across and slip the eye on to the second hook. Adjust the gathers.

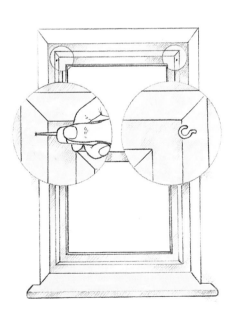

1 **Fixing the hooks** Decide on the position of the hooks and mark them with a pencil. Use the bradawl to make a pilot hole at the pencil marks. Screw hooks into the wood, finishing with them running vertically.

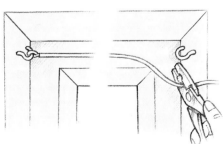

2 **Cutting the wire to fit** Screw one of the screw eyes into one end of the wire and slip it on to a hook. Stretch it tightly across to the other hook and mark the length. Cut the wire off at the marked point.

Tip

TIGHT FIT
If your tension rod is a very tight fit, use a pallet knife to ease it into place.

Stretch curtains for a door

Where a glazed door opens inwards, it is often not possible to hang curtains above the frame – a neat answer is to fix the sheer curtains to the windows only. A panel of fabric, with a casing at the top and bottom, can be slotted on to a pair of wires fixed above and below the glass. If the panel is cut to twice the width of the wire, the result is soft gathers of fabric held in place over the glass.

You can also use this technique to make a pretty show of ruched fabric on a screen or inside the glass or wire panels of cupboard doors – ideal in a bedroom or bathroom, and also for a country-style kitchen.

You will need

- ◆ Fabric
- ◆ Matching thread
- ◆ Four screws and four screw-in hooks per curtain
- ◆ Two sets of stretch wires per curtain
- ◆ Tape measure
- ◆ Pins
- ◆ Scissors

1 Measuring for wires The curtains should extend a little beyond the glass on either side (bear in mind any handles or projecting hinges) and at least 2.5cm (1in) above and below the glass to ensure that the stitching line of the casing does not show through to the other side. Measure and mark required width and length.

2 Inserting screw hooks Make sure that the area of the wood that you want to fix the wire to is both strong and thick enough to take the screw part of the screw hooks. Insert the screw hooks following step **1**, *Fixing plastic-covered wire*, given on the previous page.

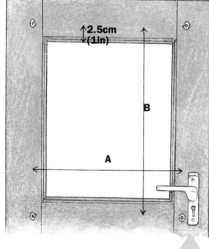

3 Measuring and cutting out Measure across the width from hook to hook (**A**), double it and add 4cm (1½in). Measure down the length from a top hook to a bottom hook (**B**) and add 14cm (5½in). Cut a piece of fabric to this size.

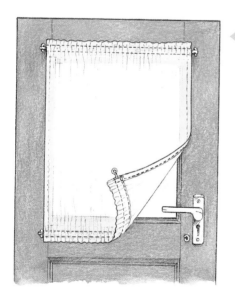

4 Making the casings To hem sides, press under a double 1cm (⅜in) hem on each long edge. Stitch close to fold. At top and bottom edges, press under a double 3.5cm (1⅜in) hem for casings. Stitch close to fold. Stitch a second line 2cm (¾in) away.

5 Hanging the curtain Slip one eye of the top wire on to one of the hooks at the top of the window. Then push the other end of the wire through the casing at the top of the curtain, gathering the fabric as necessary. Pull the wire taut and slip the eye over the hook on the opposite side. Repeat to attach the bottom wire to the window. Adjust the gathers to give the desired effect.

▶ *Sheer fabric, made with a deeper frilled casing and gathered directly across the panes of glass in a door, is a practical way of screening the view. A large, self-fabric bow nips the curtain in at the centre, adding a pretty touch.*

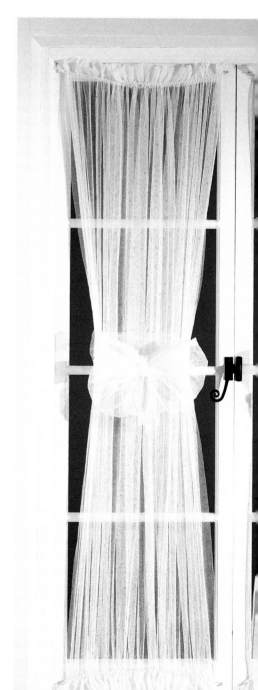

Eyelet curtains

*Get the ultimate high-tech look with the simplest possible
curtain heading – neatly spaced, gleaming eyelets, threaded on
to high-tension wire. There's very little sewing involved.*

The pared-down, sleek look of modern furnishings calls for a new functional look in curtain treatments – cool, simple and unfussy. Experiment with an eyelet kit to achieve the last word in fashionable curtains: it's easy to do, and looks sophisticated and smart in any room – it's also ideal for a shower curtain in the bathroom.

Eyelets work particularly well on unlined curtains, but you can also use them on lined curtains. On unlined curtains, the sides and bottom edge are hemmed in the usual way, while a double hem at the top edge gives body and strength – on fine fabrics, you could also add a layer of interfacing.

Thread the finished eyelet curtains on to tension wire for a smart, professional finish. Because of the high tension of the wire, the ends must be fixed to opposite walls of the room or inside the window recess, rather than on the wall that the window looks through.

Alternatively, you can slot the eyelets on to a narrow metal rod, such as a café curtain rod. Another smart option is to use a length of 10mm (⅜in) or 13mm (½in) diameter tubing, fixed in place with end sockets.

▼ *Delicate, translucent curtains threaded on to a fine wire make the most of these tall windows. With such a clear and uncluttered style of room, the overall look is elegant and understated.*

Making an unlined eyelet curtain

Eyelet curtains do not need as much fullness as tape-headed curtains – allow just one and a half times the window width. The double hem at the top edge needs to be deep enough to take the eyelets comfortably – allow for at least twice the diameter of the eyelets.

The eyelets should be spaced about 15cm (6in) apart. To decide how many you need, work out the width of each curtain, then divide the total width by 15cm (6in) and add one. This gives the minimum number of eyelets you need, but it's a good idea to buy a few extra in case you spoil any.

Make sure your eyelets have a large enough diameter to slip easily on to the wire or rod, otherwise they will not move freely when you draw the curtain. As a rough guide, tension wires require eyelets with an inner diameter of at least 15mm (⅝in). For a 10mm (⅜in) diameter rod,

the inner diameter of the eyelets should be at least 20mm (¾in). Department stores sell eyelet kits, but you may find it more difficult to get larger sizes – try some of the more specialist outlets, such as yacht chandlers, leatherwork suppliers or craft material shops.

Eyelets come in two halves, with a form (like a shaped plate) and a die (a protruding metal shape) which keep the eyelets in shape while you hammer them together, sandwiching the fabric between. Make sure that the head of your hammer is larger than the eyelet diameter. Work on a firm surface like a chopping board or a woodworking bench: you have to use quite a lot of force when hammering, and may damage a delicate surface. Some kits also have a punch tool for cutting holes in the fabric; otherwise the holes are cut with small, sharp scissors.

You will need

- ◆ Curtain fabric
- ◆ Interfacing (optional)
- ◆ Matching thread
- ◆ Dressmaker's pencil
- ◆ Eyelet kit
- ◆ Hammer
- ◆ Tension wire or narrow curtain rod
- ◆ Pair of small, sharp scissors (optional)

1 Measuring up With the rod or tension wire in position (see overleaf), and referring to pages 13–14, measure the window and work out the amount of fabric you require, allowing for a double hem at the top with a depth at least twice the diameter of the eyelets.

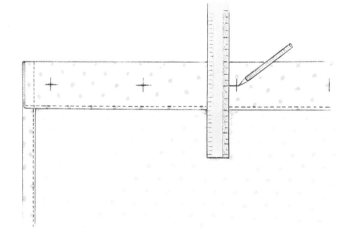

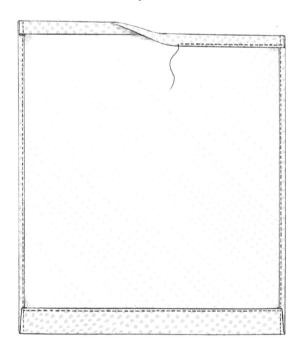

2 Hemming the curtain Make up and hem the sides and base as on pages 17–18, but take a narrow, double 1cm (⅜in) hem at the sides. At the top edge, press under a hem measuring twice the diameter of the eyelets; if necessary, apply interfacing to the wrong side of the turning to reinforce the fabric. Turn under the same amount again, then pin and stitch close to the fold.

3 Marking the positions On the wrong side of the top hem, measure 2.5cm (1in) in from each side edge and mark with a short line. Mark across it the exact centre of the hem depth, forming a small cross. Divide the remaining space equally, marking it in the same way.

4 Cutting the holes Wrong side up, centre the eyelet kit cutting tool over the first cross and strike firmly with the hammer two or three times. If you prefer, or if there is no cutting tool provided, draw around the inner hole of an eyelet and snip out the circle with small, sharp scissors. Repeat for all the crosses.

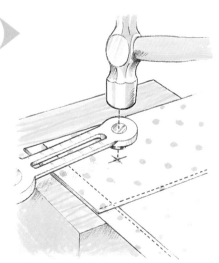

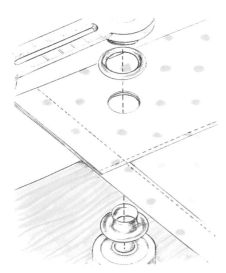

5 **Inserting the first eyelet** Place the form, shaped side up, on the surface, with the deep half of an eyelet on it, shank uppermost. Ease the first hole (wrong side up) over the shank. Place the other half of the eyelet, smooth side up, on top, and insert the die into the shank.

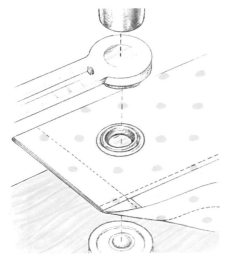

6 **Completing the eyelets** Strike the die two or three times firmly with the hammer, so the shank opens up and locks firmly round the other half. Repeat for all the remaining eyelets.

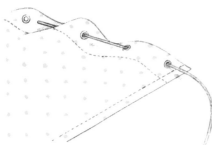

7 **Hanging the curtain** Working from the right side, push one end of the wire or rod through the first eyelet, and back out through the next. Continue in this way to the end. Fix the other end of the rod or wire, and adjust the folds of the curtain.

An ethereal swathe of spotted voile seems to hang in the air. As tension wire is so unobtrusive, it particularly suits fine fabrics.

Putting up a tension wire

Tension wire kits are available from some department stores. The kit should contain a length of steel wire, about 5m (or just over 16ft) long, two sockets with caps, and two clamps with an Allen key to tighten them.

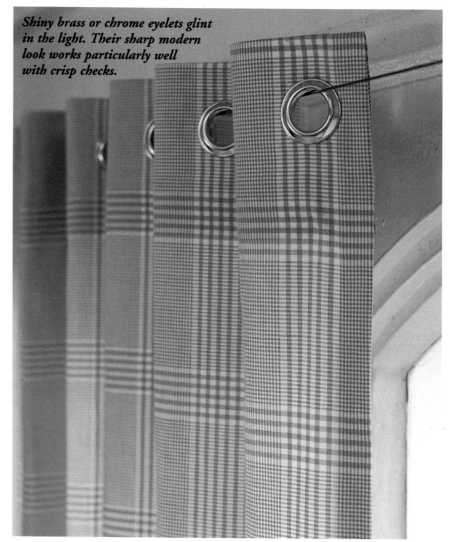

Shiny brass or chrome eyelets glint in the light. Their sharp modern look works particularly well with crisp checks.

You will need

- ◆ **Tension wire kit**
- ◆ **Two 38mm (1¹⁄₂in) No 8 countersunk screws**
- ◆ **Two rawlplugs**
- ◆ **Drill (for masonry)**
- ◆ **Screwdriver**
- ◆ **Pliers**

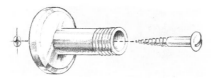

1 Fixing the brackets Measure and mark the desired height on opposite walls. Drill and plug holes at the marks and insert the screws through the socket shanks to secure them to the wall.

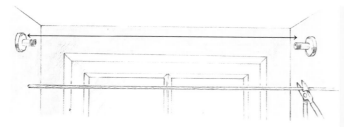

2 Cutting the wire For the exact wire length, measure from the beginning of the thread on the end of each socket shank. Cut the wire to this length with pliers.

3 Securing ends Insert each end first into the rounded end of a cap, then into the wider hole of one of the small clamps. Tighten the fixing screw with the Allen key.

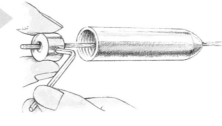

4 Completing the tension wire Thread the eyelet curtain on to the wire (see previous page). Screw each cap on to its socket, as tight as you can.

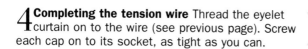

Using steel wire

Instead of a tension wire kit, you can use a length of steel wire and two steel screw eyes. Fix one screw eye in place, and half screw the other one in position. Thread the wire through the curtain eyelets and then through the eyes, using pliers to twist it back on itself to secure it. Finish screwing in the second screw eye; use pliers or insert a screwdriver into the eye for leverage. The extra turns give tension to the wire.

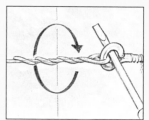

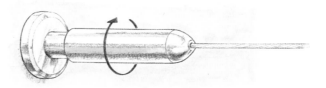

Tab headings

*The clean, functional look of tab curtain headings makes them
ideal for today's simple, uncluttered room styles; they draw attention to
a stylish pole, and are economical on fabric too.*

Tab-headed curtains have a series of loops, or strips, of fabric sewn into the top edge. The loops are simply slotted over the pole to hang the curtain. The curtains are not gathered up in the usual way – the spaces between the tabs allow a certain amount of fullness, but not as much as on standard gathered curtains. This makes tab-headed drapes more economical on fabric, giving you the scope to use a slightly more expensive cloth if desired.

A tab heading is an ideal finish for cafe curtains, which cover half the window, and it works equally well on full-length curtains. However, frequent opening and closing of tab-headed curtains may cause the fabric to wear as it rubs along the pole. To prevent this, keep the curtains pulled across at the top, and drape them back using tiebacks placed high up the window sides to allow maximum light into the room.

Choosing fabrics

You can use a tab heading for curtains made from any type of fabric and it's suitable for both lined or unlined curtains. Tabs work well with thick, chunky textures as the fabric hangs down in loose, informal folds rather than tight gathers; and they add a crisp, contemporary touch to floaty voiles or lace. Unlined calico or ticking looks elegantly simple in this style.

You can use the main curtain fabric for the tabs, or opt for a contrast to highlight one of the colours in the fabric design. For a speedy and decorative variation, buy a toning ribbon or braid for the tabs.

◄ *Self-fabric tab loops enhance the
simple, unadorned charm of
unlined, linen-look drapes, and set
off the sculptural lines of the
wrought iron pole.*

Making a simple tab heading

These steps show how to add a tab heading to unlined curtains. The curtains' top edge is strengthened with an interfaced band, which encloses the tab ends. There must be enough tabs to support the curtain – a space of two tab widths or less between each tab is recommended.

Measuring up

Fix the pole in place, making sure that it is at least 8cm (3¼in) above the top of the window to accommodate the tabs. Measure up for the curtains as on page 13, measuring from 3cm (1¼in) below the pole to the length you require.

Calculating fabric amounts

To the length measurement add 11.5cm (4⅝in) for the hem and top turning – this is the required **cut length** of the curtain. To this length add 10cm (4in) for the top facings, and for self tabs add the required tab length (*see step 2 below*) – this is the **total length**.

To calculate the number of fabric widths you need, multiply the width of the window by one and a half, divide by the width of your chosen fabric and round up the answer. Then multiply the total length by the number of fabric widths to find the total amount of fabric required.

You will need

- ◆ Furnishing fabric
- ◆ Mediumweight fusible interfacing
- ◆ Matching sewing threads
- ◆ Tape measure
- ◆ Scissors and pins

1 Cutting the curtains and facing Cutting straight across the width of the fabric, cut lengths of fabric equal to the **cut length** described above. Cut the required number of widths. For the facing, cut 10cm (4in) deep strips across the width of the fabric. Cut one for each width of curtain you are using. Cut exactly the same number of interfacing strips, 1cm (⅜in) smaller all round than the facing strips.

2 Cutting the tabs Decide how wide you want the finished tabs to be – usually 5-7.5cm (2-3in). Measure the curtain top for the number of tabs, allowing a maximum space of two tab widths between each. To work out the length of the tabs, measure around the pole and add 8cm (3¼in). Cut tab strips to the required length and twice as wide as the finished tab width, plus 2cm (¾in) for seam allowances.

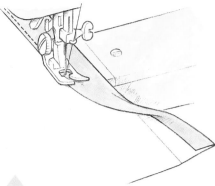

3 Making up the curtains Join fabric widths where necessary to make up the curtains. Turn 1cm (⅜in), then 2cm (¾in), to the wrong side, down the sides of each curtain. Press and stitch close to the inner fold.

◀ *When tab-headed curtains are slightly parted and drawn back, the fabric hangs elegantly in full pleats.*

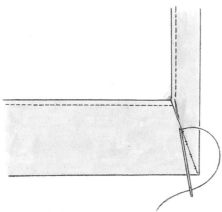

4 Turning up the hem Turn under 2.5cm (1in) then 7.5cm (3in) along the bottom edge and press. Fold the corners of the hem in at an angle at each end until they align with the side hems. Machine stitch along the hem close to the fold, right up to the side hem. To finish, slipstitch neatly along the folded corners.

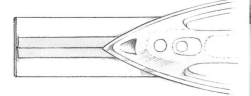

5 Making the tabs With the right sides together, fold each tab in half lengthways and stitch the long edge, taking a 1cm (³⁄₈in) seam allowance. Centre the seam and press, with allowances open. Turn right side out and press again.

6 Positioning the tabs Lay out the main curtain fabric with the right side facing up. Pin a folded tab to each end, with the raw ends matching the raw edge of the curtain. Fold the remaining tabs and pin and tack them evenly in between.

7 Preparing the facing Apply interfacing to the wrong side of the facing strip. If there is more than one fabric width in the curtain, join facing strips to match. Neaten one long edge of the facing, then turn up to form a 2.5cm (1in) hem and stitch close to the neatened edge.

8 Attaching the facing With the wrong side facing up, and the raw edges matching, lay the facing over the tabs. Tack, then stitch across the curtain top, through the facing, the tabs and the main fabric, taking a 1.5cm (⁵⁄₈in) seam allowance. Trim the ends of the tabs, layering them and clipping diagonally across the corners to reduce bulk.

▲ *For a child's room, make the tab heading from two or more plain fabrics and decorate it with bright felt shapes.*

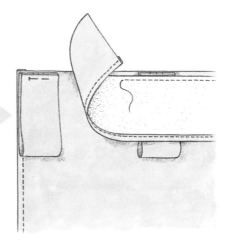

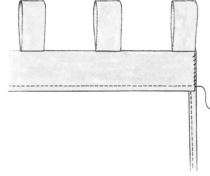

9 Finishing off Turn and press the facing so that it lies against the wrong side of the curtain. Press under the raw edges of the facing at each end of the curtain and slipstitch them to the curtain's side hem.

Making a pointed tab heading

For a decorative tab heading, the front end of the tab is finished with a neat point, lapped over the front of the curtain and fastened with a button. Make a feature of the buttons by choosing ones that stand out from the fabric.

1 Cutting out Measure up for the tabs as in *step 2* of *Making a simple tab heading*, but add an extra 7cm (2¾in) to the length for the overlap. Cut out one tab and test the length by wrapping it around the pole and lapping it on to a piece of fabric. Adjust the length, if necessary. Cut remaining tab strips to the same size.

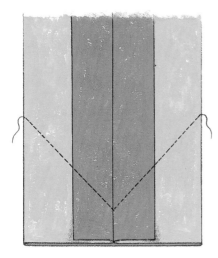

2 Stitching the point Make up the tabs as in *step 5* of *Making a simple tab heading*, but do not turn them right side out. Measure and mark the centre point of the tab, 1cm (³⁄₈in) up from the raw edge. Measure and mark 4cm (1½in) up from the raw edge on each side edge. Starting at one side edge, stitch in a straight line to the centre point. Pivot the fabric and stitch to the other side.

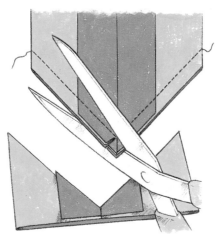

3 Turning to the right side Trim the fabric to 6mm (¼in) from the stitching line and cut away a 'V' of fabric at the point. Turn the tab right side out and press.

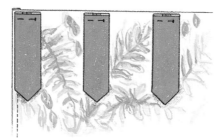

4 Attaching the tabs Position the tabs as for *Making a simple tab heading*, *step 6*, but pin only the raw end to the top of the curtain, leaving the pointed end free. Check that the centre seam on each tab lies against the right side of the fabric.

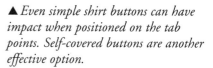

▲ *Even simple shirt buttons can have impact when positioned on the tab points. Self-covered buttons are another effective option.*

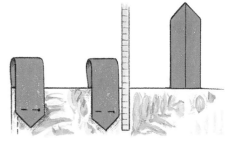

5 Finishing off Add the facing as for *steps 7-9* of *Making a simple tab heading*. Fold the tab strips over to the right side of the curtain's top edge. Pin them in place, making sure the points are all 7cm (2¾in) below the top edge. Check that the curtain pole fits through the tabs. Stitch a button on to each tab, stitching through the tab and the curtain.

Tip

LIGHTWEIGHT FABRICS
If you are using a lightweight fabric to make the tabs, it's a good idea to strengthen them with lightweight fusible interfacing.

Novelty curtain tabs

Unusual tab headings add individuality to your room, and focus attention on a stylish pole as well. Use sharply contrasting colours or patterns to make the most of the feature.

Triangular or diamond-shaped curtain tabs provide sparky interest in a contemporary room, and they are the perfect way to remodel an old pair of curtains. They add about 7.5-10cm (3-4in) to the height of the curtain, and look best with very little fullness in the width – so you can use them to adapt drapes to fit a larger window.

The strong, clean-cut shape of the tabs complements any number of colour and pattern combinations. You could offset plain calico curtains with natural linen tabs; or highlight a single colour in a striped curtain – adding black tabs to black and white ticking, for instance. Alternatively, pick out a crisp leaf green to enliven a blowsy rose print.

Make the tabs in a firmly woven, robust fabric, choosing a colour that contrasts sharply with the curtain fabric. Line them with either self fabric, your curtain fabric, or even a third contrasting fabric.

The tabs featured on these pages are big and bold, with a finished top width of about 15cm (6in) – with tabs as large as this, you will only need to make four or five per width, depending on the width of your chosen curtain fabric.

◀ *The handsome shape of these tabs is shown off to full advantage by slim curtains. They are just one and a half times the width of the pole, giving a simple and streamlined look. You could even make yours a little less wide – it's better to err on the narrow side, as any hint of puffiness could contradict the clean lines of the tabs.*

Making a diamond tab heading

These bold, diamond-shaped tabs are made and attached in a similar way to the simple tab heading featured on pages 34–36. The ones shown here are lined with self fabric, but you could line them with your curtain fabric or a contrasting fabric, if you prefer. The curtains are unlined, and the tops are supported by a band of self (curtain) fabric, stiffened with fusible interfacing.

Calculating fabric amounts

Fix the pole, positioning it so that the top is at least 8cm (3¼in) above the top of the window, to accommodate the tabs.

Measure up for the curtains as shown on page 13, but measure from 3cm (1¼in) below the pole to the length required. To this add 11.5cm (4⅝in) for the hem and top turning – this is the **cut length**. Then add 15cm (6in) for the top facings. If you are lining the tabs with curtain fabric, allow extra for this: you will need 36-40cm (14½-15¾in) for four tabs. This is the **total length**.

To calculate the required number of fabric widths, allow a scant one and a half times the pole length, divided by the fabric width. Round up the answer, then multiply the total length by the number of fabric widths to find the total amount of fabric required.

You will need

◆ Curtain fabric

◆ Contrasting fabric for tabs

◆ Contrasting lining fabric for tabs (optional)

◆ Mediumweight fusible interfacing

◆ Matching threads

◆ Paper, pencil and ruler

◆ Dressmaker's chalk

1 Cutting the curtains and facings Cut the required number of fabric widths to the cut length, as described above. Cutting across the fabric width, cut the same number of 15cm (6in) deep strips for the facing. Then cut the same number of interfacing strips, but cut them 1cm (⅜in) smaller all round than the fabric strips.

2 Making the curtains Following pages 34–35, steps **3-4**, make up the curtains and hem the lower and side edges. Fuse an interfacing strip centrally to the wrong side of each fabric interfacing strip. If there is more than one fabric width in the curtain, join the facing strips to match. Then neaten one long edge of the facing. Turn up the same edge to form a 2.5cm (1in) hem and stitch close to the neatened edge.

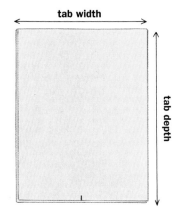

3 Starting the tab pattern Decide on the finished width and depth of the tabs – the ones shown here are 15cm (6in) wide and 18cm (7in) deep. Cut a piece of paper this width and twice the depth. Fold it in half widthways, and mark the centre of the cut edge.

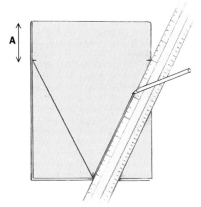

4 Cutting the shape Measure round the pole and divide this by two (**A**). Make a mark this distance down from the fold on each edge of the paper. Draw a straight line from each of these marks to the centre mark at the bottom. Cut along the lines.

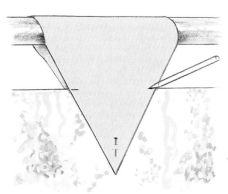

5 Marking the pattern Check pattern by wrapping it around the pole and pinning it to a piece of the fabric. Mark the point on each side of the pattern where it overlaps curtain top. Using the pattern, and adding 1cm (⅜in) all round for seams, cut two fabric pieces for each tab (alternatively, cut second fabric piece for each tab from curtain fabric or another contrasting fabric).

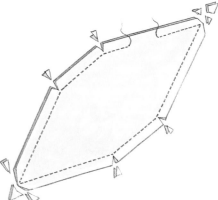

6 Making the tabs For each tab, pin the two pieces right sides together; taking a 1cm (⅜in) seam allowance, stitch all round, leaving a 5cm (2in) opening for turning. Trim the seam allowances, and clip close at all the points to reduce bulk. Turn the tab to the right side and press, pushing out the points with a knitting needle or bodkin. Slipstitch the opening closed.

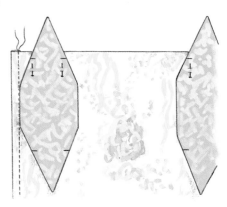

7 Positioning the tabs Mark the overlap points, as on the pattern, on the right side of each half of the tabs. Lay the curtain flat, with the right side facing up. Then, right side up, position the back half of a tab close to each end of the curtain top, with the overlap marks 1.5cm (⅝in) below the raw edge; pin. Space the other tabs evenly between, and pin in place.

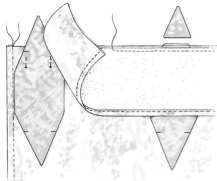

8 Adding the facing With the wrong side of the facing up, and matching the raw edges, lay the facing over the tabs. Tack, then stitch across the curtain top, taking a 1.5cm (⅝in) seam. Trim off the pointed ends of the tabs, layering the seams to reduce bulk. Then turn the facing, press it and finish the ends, following step **9** on page 35.

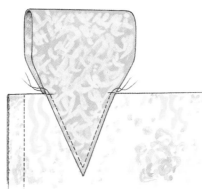

9 Completing the tabs Fold each tab point over the front of the curtain, matching the overlap marks, and pin to hold. Topstitch through all the layers, close to the edge of the tab, working from the top of the curtain, down to the point and up the other side.

▲ *A traditional floral curtain gains a contemporary twist with the addition of sharp, diamond-shaped tabs. For this variation on the diamond shape, make the tab pattern in the same way, but in step 4 draw the straight line from the folded edge itself to the marked centre bottom. If you wish to give the tabs extra definition by adding piping, tack it in place on to the main fabric piece before assembling the tab (see step 6). Pivot the needle at the corners, and clip the seam allowances carefully to reduce bulk.*

Making a triangle tab heading

These striking triangular-shaped tabs make the most of a simple geometric shape to create a stylish and unusual curtain heading. Although the tabs are just another version of the diamond shape shown on the previous page – using half the diamond shape to make the triangle – the contrast lining gives a totally different effect, while the bold buttons sharpen the look.

You will need all the materials listed on the previous page, plus a button for each tab in a contrast colour.

1 Preparing the curtain Fix up the pole, measure up and calculate the fabric requirements, as described on the previous page. Then, following steps **1-2**, make up the curtains, hem the side and lower edges and prepare the facing strips. Decide on the width and depth of the finished tab – the ones shown below are 15cm (6in) wide and 20cm (8in) deep. Cut a piece of paper to this size. Mark the centre of the lower edge, then draw a line from each top corner to this mark. Cut along the lines.

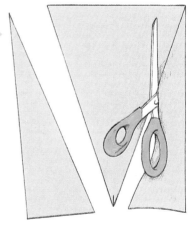

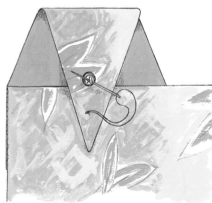

2 Making the tabs Using the pattern and allowing an extra 1.5cm (⅝in) all round for seams, cut the required number of tabs in fabric and contrast lining. Pin the fabric and lining of each tab right sides together; stitch the two diagonal edges. Trim the seams and clip the corners, turn out and press.

3 Positioning the tabs Right side of curtain facing up, lining side of tab facing down, and raw edges matching, pin a tab at each end of the curtain top. Space the other tabs evenly between and pin in place.

4 Finishing Following step **8** on the previous page, apply and neaten the facing. Fold over the point of the tab, so that it overlaps the top of the curtain, and pin it in place. Centre a button over the point and stitch it on through all the layers, securing the point of the tab at the same time.

Tie-on curtains

*Today's look of simple practicality is perfectly echoed by
curtains attached to a pole with ties, adding detail at the top
of the curtain with a functional but decorative look.*

◀ *Fabric ties are a good
choice for any curtains which
have a large, bold design,
such as this blue and yellow
checked fabric, where a more
conventional heading might
look rather fussy. Here, the
tie-on heading complements
the modern look of the room.*

Stitching fabric ties to the top edge of a curtain makes an interesting alternative to a conventional heading, attached to rings on a pole. Instead of hooking the curtains on to rings, pairs of ties are spaced along the top of the curtain, and tied around the pole. You can make the ties thick or thin, long or short; to stand up in a chunky knot, or fall gracefully in front of the curtain like ribbons; you can even tie them in a series of pretty bows. Make sure you cut them long enough to tie securely around the pole, and wide enough to support the weight of the curtain.

Like tab-headed curtains, tie-on curtains are economical on fabric. They need less fullness than standard curtain treatments – you can cut the curtain width to just one and a half times the pole length. Use the same fabric as the curtain for the ties, or choose a contrasting colour – you could achieve a rainbow effect, for example, by picking out different colours from a print.

The following pages show you how to make unlined tie-on curtains.

Making unlined tie-on curtains

As tie-on curtains hang below the curtain pole, the brackets should be positioned to hold the pole at least 5cm (2in) above the window frame to ensure the drapes block out light and draughts effectively.

Unlined tie-on curtains are made in the same way as tab-headed curtains, with a stiffened band or facing along the top, into which the ties are inserted. To help you decide on the width and length of your ties, experiment by tying strips of scrap fabric in various widths around the pole. Narrow ties should be spaced about 13-15cm (5¼-6in) apart; wider ones can be up to 20cm (8in) apart. As a guide, 2.5cm (1in) wide ties cut 30cm (12in) long will have 7.5cm (3in) ends after knotting round a 2cm (¾in) diameter pole, and can be spaced about 15cm (6in) apart.

Fabric quantities

Measure up for the curtains as on page 13, measuring from 3cm (1¼in) below the pole to the length you require. Add 11.5cm (4⅝in) to the finished length measurement for the hem and top turnings to get the **cut length** of the curtains. Add 10cm (4in) for the facing and, for self-fabric ties, add the required tie length plus 2.5cm (1in), to get the **total length**. Multiply by the number of widths you need to find the total amount of fabric required.

You will need

- ◆ **Furnishing fabric**
- ◆ **Contrast fabric for ties (optional)**
- ◆ **Mediumweight fusible interfacing**
- ◆ **Matching sewing thread**
- ◆ **Tape measure**
- ◆ **Pins and scissors**

1 Cutting out curtains and facing
Cut out the curtains and the facing as in step **1** on page 34. Join widths of fabric together as necessary to make up each required curtain width. Prepare the facing following the instructions in step **7** on page 35.

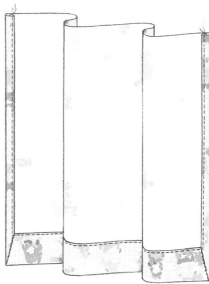

2 Hemming side and bottom edges
On each side edge, turn under a 1cm (⅜in) then 2cm (¾in) double hem; press and then stitch the hem close to the fold. At the bottom edge, turn under a 2.5cm (1in) then 7.5cm (3in) double hem; press and stitch the hem close to the fold, turning the corners in and slipstitching them in place by hand.

◀ *Why hide an attractive, wrought-iron pole, when you can show it off to full effect simply by securing the fabric ties to curtain rings so that the curtains hang below the pole?*

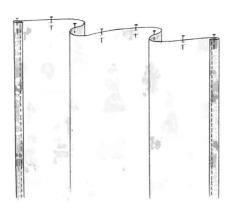

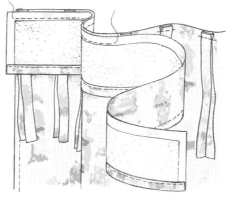

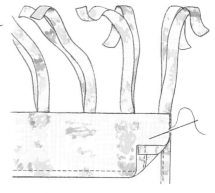

3 **Marking the tie positions** Placing one pair of ties at each outer edge, decide on the position of each pair and mark with a pin along the top edge of one curtain. Count the pins to see how many pairs of ties you need to make.

4 **Cutting out the ties** For each pair of curtain ties, cut two strips of fabric twice the finished tie width plus 2cm (³⁄₄in), by the finished tie length plus 2.5cm (1in).

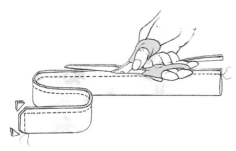

5 **Stitching the ties** With right sides together, fold each tie in half lengthways. Stitch a 1cm (³⁄₈in) seam along the raw edge and one short edge. Trim the seam to 6mm (¹⁄₄in) and clip corners, then turn through to the right side and press.

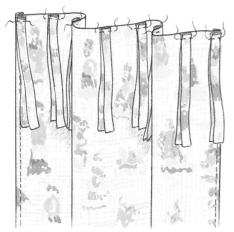

6 **Placing the ties** Match the raw edges of each pair of ties and centre them at each pinned position on the right side of the curtain. Tack in place, with raw edges level with the top of the curtain.

7 **Adding facing** With wrong side of facing up and raw edges matching, lay facing over ties. Tack, then stitch across curtain top through all layers, taking a 1.5cm (⁵⁄₈in) seam allowance. Trim ends of ties, layering them and clipping corners to reduce bulk.

8 **Finishing off the top edge** Turn and press the facing to the wrong side of the curtain. Press under the raw edges of the facing at each end of the curtain and slipstitch them to the side hem.

Narrow fabric ties give a more delicate heading treatment. For a fully coordinated look, choose fabric from a complementary range to make matching soft furnishings.

Bordered tie-on curtains

Stitch the curtain ties into a snappy top border to give them more impact, then carry the border right round the edge of the curtain like a picture frame. You can create wonderful effects with contrasting fabrics – add plain borders to busy prints, for example, or use bias stripes to jazz up plain curtains; make the ties in the border fabric or add another contrast colour. The ties are made in the same way as on the previous page. You'll need the same materials as for the tie-on curtains, plus fabric for the border. These instructions are for a 5cm (2in) border.

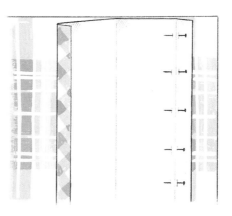

1 Cutting out the curtains Measure up as on page 13, measuring from 3cm (1¼in) below the pole to the length you require. Cut the required number of widths to exactly this length and join as necessary.

2 Cutting the borders *For each curtain:* cut two side border strips the curtain length by 13cm (5¼in) wide; one bottom border strip the curtain width plus 4cm (1½in) by 13cm (5¼in) wide; and one top border strip the length of the bottom strip by 16cm (6¼in) wide.

3 Marking tie positions Cut top border in half lengthways to form a front and back border strip. Starting and finishing 2cm (¾in) in from each end, mark tie positions with pins along upper edge of front strip. Count pins to see how many pairs of ties you need.

▼ *A clever design option, here the gingham has been cut on the bias to create heading ties and a coordinating border for these large-checked curtains.*

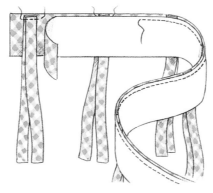

4 Making the ties Cut out and make up the required number of ties as in steps **4-5** on previous page. With raw edges matching, pin and tack one pair of ties to right side of the front border at each pin. Right sides together, pin back strip to front strip, sandwiching the ties between. Stitch along the top edge, taking a 1.5cm (⅝in) seam.

5 Pressing the borders Press under a 1.5cm (⅝in) seam allowance on the long edges of each border piece. Wrong sides together, press each border in half lengthways.

6 Stitching the side borders Open out the pressed seam allowance on one edge of one of the side borders. With right sides together, place the raw edge of the border 3.5cm (1⅜in) in from one side edge of the curtain. Pin, then stitch in place along the crease of seam allowance. Repeat with the other side border.

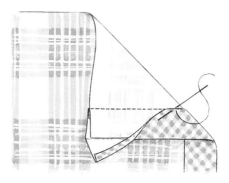

7 Slipstitching the side borders Fold each side border to the wrong side of the curtain, enclosing the raw edges. Slipstitch the fold to the previous stitched line so that no stitches show through to the front.

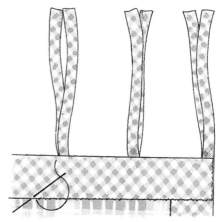

8 Adding top and bottom borders Centre the top and bottom borders on the upper and lower edges of the curtain, and stitch them in place, as in steps **7-8** on previous page, positioning them 2cm (¾in) in from each end.

Iron-on curtain headings

*Whiz up the fastest ever pair of stylish curtains without
a single stitch – all you need is your iron and ironing board,
when you take advantage of the latest heading tapes.*

With the clever, new timesaving products for soft furnishings, making curtains is so easy. Fusible tapes and interfacings – which stick firmly to the fabric when you apply a hot iron – make sewing completely unnecessary. So, if you feel like a break from your machine, and want to produce a quick curtain, consider these no-sew options. You can choose from gathered or pencil pleat headings with an iron-on finish, while iron-on hemming tape makes fast work of side and bottom hems.

Most cotton, polyester and polyester mix fabrics are suitable for no-sew tapes. Avoid velvet or fabrics with a special finish, such as glazed chintz or flame-proofed fabrics, as they will be altered by the pressing required.

▼ *The tab-heading tape allows you to make up and hang professional looking tabs, without sewing a stitch.*

Making the no-sew curtains

The no-sew curtain kit contains enough hemming and heading tape for a pair of curtains up to 137cm (54in) long, with one and a half fabric widths each. If you want to make longer curtains, you can buy extra hemming tape separately.

For measuring up, calculating fabric amounts and cutting out curtains, see pages 11–17. Before fusing the tapes in place, read the manufacturer's instructions carefully and set your iron to the steam specified setting.

Although the method is quick, it is not instantaneous, so you need to set up the iron in a comfortable position – you could set yourself up to sit comfortably in front of the TV, for instance.

You will need

- ◆ **Furnishing fabric**
- ◆ **No-sew curtain kit**
- ◆ **Tape measure**
- ◆ **Steam iron**
- ◆ **Cotton pressing cloth**
- ◆ **Dressmaker's pencil**

1 Measuring up and cutting out Follow the steps on pages 11–17 to measure up and cut out the required widths for the curtains.

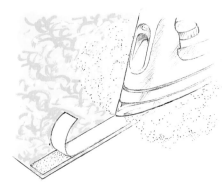

2 Applying tape to the first width Lay the first panel of fabric right side up. Cut a piece of hemming tape to the fabric length and lay it, honeycomb side down, along the edge to be joined. Press the iron on to the tape; work down the whole length, lifting and then pressing down with the iron, rather than sliding it along the fabric. Leave it to cool, then peel off the backing tape.

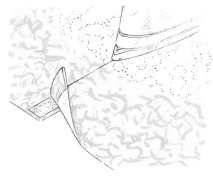

3 Joining widths On the next fabric panel, press under 1.5cm (⅝in) on the edge to be joined. Right side up, lay pressed edge over the hemming tape, carefully matching any pattern. Press firmly with the steam iron to bond the two pieces together. Repeat for other widths, as necessary.

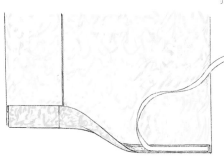

4 Neatening the base Press under 2.5cm (1in) then 7.5cm (3in) at the lower edge. Following step **2**, fuse the hemming tape to the smaller hem; peel off the tape backing paper and press the rest of the hem in place, sandwiching the tape between the fabric layers. Fuse in place.

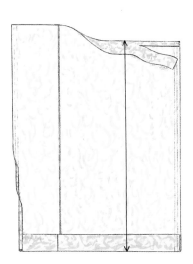

5 Pressing side hems and top edge On each side of the curtain, press under a double 1.2cm (½in) hem; then open it out again. Measure the finished curtain length *up* from the bottom edge, and press over at this point; trim away excess to 2.5cm (1in).

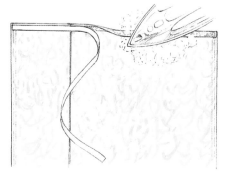

6 Neatening the top edge Apply the hemming tape to the wrong side of the top turning, peel off the backing and fuse in place, as in step **2**.

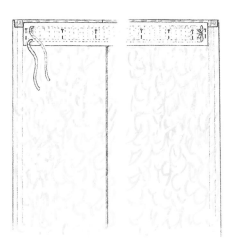

7 Positioning the heading tape Cut a length of heading tape the width of the curtain plus about 7.5cm (3in). Lay it across the top of the curtain, 3mm (⅛in) down from the top fold, so that it extends the same amount each edge. On pencil pleat tape, the yellow line should be along the lower edge.

8 Preparing the cords *At leading edge of curtain:* pick out 5cm (2in) of the draw cords and knot them close to the tape. Trim the cords and tape to within 6mm (¼in) of the knots, and line up cut edge with inner foldline at side edge. Pin tape in place. *At outer edge of curtain:* pick out the draw cords to 1.5cm (⅝in) inside the inner side edge foldline and leave ends loose. Trim tape level with foldline.

▲ *Give yourself a break from sewing and press together a pair of simple, sill-length curtains. The method is ideal for use on light to mediumweight fabrics that do not require a stitched-in lining. The pencil pleat version is shown here.*

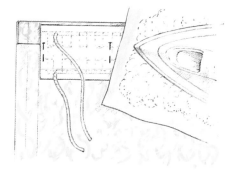

9 **Fusing the heading tape** Place a dry pressing cloth on top of the tape and press firmly with the iron to fuse the tape in place. Re-press any areas that don't adhere the first time.

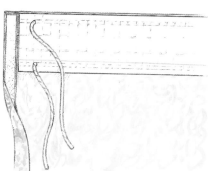

10 **Fusing the side hems** Apply hemming tape to the inner fold of one side hem. Peel off the backing and refold; press again to fuse. Repeat with the other side hem.

11 **Hanging the curtains** To pleat the curtains, hold the free cords in one hand and the top of the curtain in the other hand. Gently push the heading along the cords until the fabric is neatly pleated to the required width. Insert the curtain hooks and hang curtain in place at your window.

No-sew tab top curtains

All you need to make stylish tab curtains is a no-sew tab kit, hemming tape, plus fabric for the curtains, tabs and self-cover buttons. You can make 10 tabs from one kit – that's enough for a pair of curtains with one and a half fabric widths each. If you want to stiffen the curtain tops, use fusible buckram rather than the hemming tape to neaten the top edges.

You will need

- ◆ **Fabric for making one pair of no-sew curtains**
- ◆ **Fabric for tabs and buttons**
- ◆ **No-sew tab kit**
- ◆ **Hemming tape**
- ◆ **Fusible buckram (optional)**
- ◆ **Fray preventer (optional)**

1 Making the curtain Prepare sides and base of curtain as for *Making the no-sew curtains* on previous page, but omit heading tape. If you wish, stiffen top edge with fusible buckram.

2 Preparing the tab fabric *For each tab:* cut a strip of fabric 31 x 10cm (12¼ x 4in). Centre a buckram strip on the wrong side of one fabric strip, to prepare for making the template.

3 Drawing the template With a pencil and ruler, mark a straight line along both short edges of the fabric, extending from the buckram corners to the outside edges. Mark the centre of the short edges, and draw a line from the buckram corners to the centre marks.

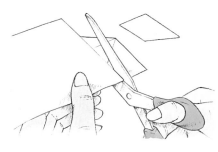

4 Shaping the strips At each short end of the fabric strip, trim the fabric just outside the lines marked in step **2**. Use this as a template to cut the other strips. If desired, seal the cut edges with liquid fray preventer.

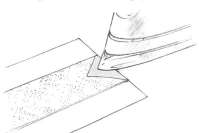

5 Fusing the ends Centre a buckram strip on the wrong side of a fabric strip. Fold the triangular fabric flaps over the buckram and fuse with the tip of a hot iron, being careful not to touch the rest of the buckram with the iron.

▼ *Extra style doesn't have to mean extra effort. This no-sew tab kit takes the toil out of creating chic tab top curtains.*

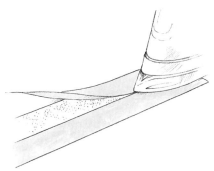

6 Fusing the sides Turn under a tiny hem along the long edges and press. Then fold the long edges over the buckram, to meet in the centre. Fuse with the iron. Repeat to fuse the ends and sides of the other tabs.

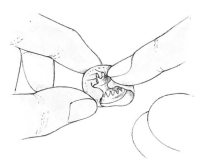

7 Covering the buttons Cut a circle of fabric for each button, using pattern supplied with kit. Pull fabric circle tightly over button, pressing it into the teeth. To assemble, push a pin through the back plate of the button, then place the back plate on the back of the button and squeeze together between finger and thumb.

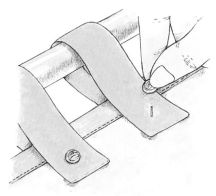

8 Securing the tabs Place a tab at each end of curtain; space the others evenly between; mark their positions. Place curtain pole on a flat surface. Lay curtain, wrong side up, just beneath it. Holding first tab in position around pole, push button pin right through front of the tab, the curtain and back of the tab; push a pin protector on to point of pin to secure button in position. Attach remaining tabs in same way.

Curtains with a frilled casing

*One of the fastest and easiest ways of hanging a curtain is
to stitch a casing at the top to take the curtain pole. A frilled
heading adds a decorative finish.*

Making a casing or slot heading is the very simplest way to hang curtains. You simply fold the fabric at the top of the curtain and sew through both layers to make the casing or slot. You can then slip a pole, rod or even curtain wire through the casing Cund hang the curtain.

This method is perfect for hanging curtains that don't need to be opened and closed, like café curtains and nets. It also works well for more formal treatments, provided you use holdbacks or tiebacks to loop the curtains away from the window during the day, instead of trying to pull them back. Fix the pole and tiebacks high up to let maximum light flood in through the window.

Any metal or wooden pole can be used. You won't need any rings; just fit

▲ *Curtains made with a casing can look grand enough for your living or dining room, with the added advantage that they are very easy to make. The stand-up frill helps to create the formal effect.*

the brackets in the usual way, push the pole through the curtain casing, and position it on the pole supports.

Casing with stand-up frill

These steps are for unlined curtains. Before you start, decide on the type and thickness of the rod or pole you are going to use, as the casing is made to fit it. The depth of the frill should be in proportion to the thickness of the pole and the curtain length; as a general rule, long curtains need a thick pole, and therefore a deep casing and frill.

Also decide how full the curtains will be – double fullness gives an attractive ruched effect and a full frill. On very full curtains, allow for a generous casing which will ruche on to the pole easily.

You will need

◆ **Curtain fabric**

◆ **Matching thread**

◆ **Tape measure**

◆ **Pins**

◆ **Tailor's chalk (optional)**

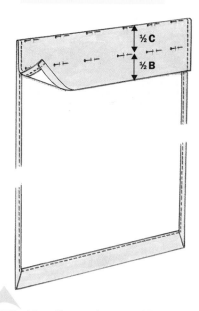

2 Planning the casing and frill depth Run the tape measure around the rod and add a minimum of 3cm (1¼in) for ease (**B**). Decide on the depth of the frill and double it (**C**).

3 Estimating fabric Add **A**, **B** and **C** together plus 11.5cm (4⅝in) for the hem allowances. This gives the total cut length of the curtain (**D**). Multiply **D** by the number of widths you are using to calculate the total amount of fabric required.

4 Cutting out and making up Cut the required number of widths to the cut length **D**. Make up the curtain as shown in steps **1-6** on page 17, taking a 10cm (4in) hem.

1 Measuring the finished length Fix the rod or pole above the window. Measure from the base of the rod or pole to the required curtain length (**A**).

▼ *This bathroom curtain, adds a pretty, softening touch to the room, while the blind does the real work of screening the window.*

5 Marking the casing and frill Press under a 1.5cm (⅝in) hem on the top raw edge. From the fold, measure and mark, with pins or tailor's chalk, the depth of the casing (½**B**), then the depth of the frill (½**C**). Fold the fabric along the frill line and press.

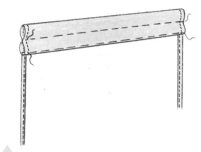

6 Stitching the casing Pin, then tack through all layers along the marked casing line and the pressed hem, from one side of the curtain to the other. Machine stitch just beside each line of tacking. (If you stitch over the tacking it is hard to remove.) Unpick the tacking.

7 Dressing the curtain Dress the curtain by sliding it over the curtain rod and adjusting the gathers. If required, secure tieback hooks or holdbacks high up on the window.

Valance-headed curtains

*A built-in valance adds definition at the top of a
curtain, without restricting the amount of light, and
shows off an attractive pole at the same time*

If you like the softening effect of a gathered valance, but yearn for a stylish pole too, the treatment for you is a valance-headed curtain, which combines both looks at once. This versatile window dressing will suit a casual, bright style and modern fabrics, or a formal, well-dressed look in a period setting.

To make a valance-headed curtain, you can either make up the valance separately, using curtain fabric or a contrasting fabric and attach it to the top of the curtain, or you can set the heading tape lower down so that the extra fabric flops forward: this method is especially effective if you use a contrast lining. For

▲ *Coffee and cream make a sophisticated ensemble. Here, plain curtains are defined with a coffee-coloured valance, and contrast borders and ties.*

extra interest, you can either shape the lower edge of the valance or trim it with a fringe.

Making valance-headed curtains

The steps below explain how to make a simple lined curtain with a valance which is cut separately and attached at the heading stage. Refer to pages 13–20 for basic instructions on making the curtain.

When deciding on the depth of the valance, work on the usual principle of one-sixth of the curtain length, but bear in mind that some of the valance depth will be taken up by the heading.

If you are making the valance from the same fabric as the curtain, it's important to match the pattern on the two layers. If you are using different fabrics, it is easier if they are the same width; if not, allow for an extra width to make up the difference.

When buying fabric for the valance, allow for the valance depth plus 10cm (4in) for each cut length of curtain. As it sits in front of the curtain, the valance does not need lining – an extra layer of fabric would add unwanted bulk.

You will need

- ◆ Curtain fabric
- ◆ Valance fabric
- ◆ Curtain lining
- ◆ Heading tape
- ◆ Matching thread
- ◆ Pins
- ◆ Measuring tape
- ◆ Curtain hooks

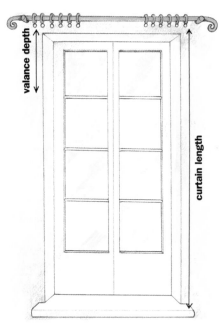

1 Measuring up Following page 13, measure the length and width of the curtains. Then decide on the depth of the valance, measuring from the top of the curtain.

2 Cutting the fabric *For the curtain:* follow steps **1-3** on page 17 to cut the same width and length in lining and curtain fabric. Join widths and press seams open. *For the valance:* add 10cm (4in) to desired valance depth, then cut the same number of widths of valance fabric as for curtain.

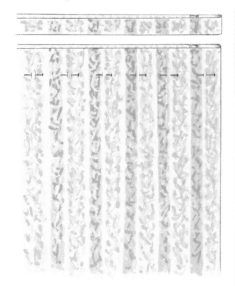

3 Making up the curtains Turn up the hems, join the lining to the fabric and finish the hem corners, as in steps **2-8** on pages 19–20. Measure the required length of the curtain from the bottom edge, and mark with pins along the width. Trim the remainder to 2.5cm (1in).

4 Making up the valance Join the valance widths to make a long strip the same width as each curtain, plus 3cm (1⅛in) at each side edge for turnings. Press the seams open.

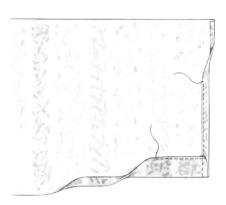

5 Hemming the valance On the side edges, press under 1cm (⅜in) then 2cm (¾in); stitch close to the inner fold. On the bottom edge, press under 2.5cm (1in) then 5cm (2in), turning in the sides of the hem slightly so they will not show from the front. Stitch close to the inner fold.

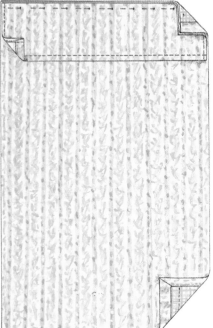

6 Applying the valance Lay one curtain, right side up, on a flat surface. Then lay the valance, right side up, on top of the curtain, matching the top and side edges; pin them together along the top edge. Treating the two layers as one, press 2.5cm (1in) to the wrong side at top edge, and open out the fold again.

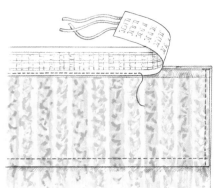

7 Positioning the heading tape Cut a piece of heading tape the width of the curtain plus 2.5cm (1in). Centre the tape right side up, on the right side of the valance, with its *lower edge* at the top and its *upper edge* just above the foldline. Pin, then stitch close to this edge through all fabric layers.

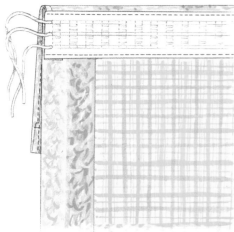

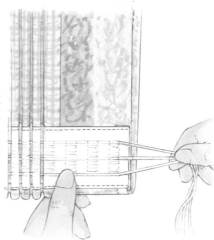

▲ On tall, narrow windows, an attached valance helps to break the line of the window into smaller sections and balance the length. Here the valance is cut separately and stitched in with the heading tape for a smart, formal look.

10 Positioning the curtain hooks Adjust the gathers evenly across the width of the curtain, then insert a curtain hook into the end pockets of the curtain tape. Fold the curtain in half and insert a hook at the centre.

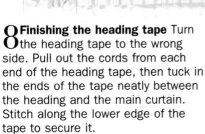

8 Finishing the heading tape Turn the heading tape to the wrong side. Pull out the cords from each end of the heading tape, then tuck in the ends of the tape neatly between the heading and the main curtain. Stitch along the lower edge of the tape to secure it.

9 Gathering the curtain Pull up the loose cord ends evenly until the curtain is gathered to the right width. Knot the cord ends near the heading tape to hold the gathers. Slip the cord tidy into the heading tape or catch the wound cord with two stitches to the top of the curtain.

11 Spacing the remaining hooks Space out the remaining curtain hooks evenly along the heading tape, every 10cm (4in) between the end and centre hooks. Finally, check that there is a track runner or curtain ring for each hook in the heading tape and hang the curtains.

Making a flop-over valance curtain

This stylish curtain is made in a single piece, then folded over at the top to create the valance. With its easy, casual look, it is ideal for a more modern room. If you wish, you can add a contrast lining for a really striking effect.

The instructions given here explain how to make a valance curtain to hang from a decorative curtain pole. You will need to use exactly the same amount of lining as fabric. Use standard gathering tape or pencil pleat tape, and gather the curtains, as here; or allow for less fullness in the width when measuring up and leave the curtains ungathered.

You will need

◆ **Curtain fabric**

◆ **Contrast lining fabric**

◆ **Matching thread**

◆ **Heading tape**

◆ **Curtain hooks**

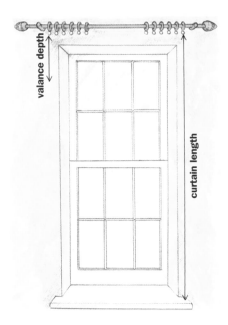

1 Measuring up Measure from the eye of the curtain ring to the desired curtain length. Then decide on the depth of the valance.

2 Cutting out *From fabric:* add curtain length and valance depth together, plus 15cm (6in) for hem and 1.5cm (⅝in) for top. Cut required number of lengths by curtain width. *From lining:* cut same number of lengths as fabric, but cut them 9cm (3½ in) shorter.

3 Seaming and hemming Join fabric and lining widths as necessary and press seams open. Turn up the hems, as in step **2** on page 19.

4 Joining the lining and fabric Lay out the curtain and lining right sides together, matching the top edges and centres or seams. Join the lining to the fabric as in step **4** on page 20.

5 Stitching the top Lay the curtain out again, wrong sides out, and match seams or centres so that the fabric wraps round to the lining side by 3cm (1¼in) on each side. Pin then stitch across the top, turn out to the right side and press.

6 Completing the curtain Finish the hem corners as in steps **6-8** on page 20. Then measure valance depth down from the top edge and mark across the width with pins. Referring to page 18, steps **8-13**, apply the heading tape just below the line of pins, then gather it up. Finally, hang the curtains, dressing the valance forward over the tape.

▲ *Make the most of a cheery contrast lining with a flop-over valance heading, which draws the eye upwards to give an impression of height.*

Straight curtain valance

Hanging across the top of a window, a gathered valance is a pretty way to conceal the curtain track and headings. It's quick to make and easy to fix on to a special valance track or pelmet shelf.

Essentially, a valance is just a very short curtain, fixed across the full width at the top of the window. It is gathered with curtain heading tape, so you can choose different styles to suit your room.

You can make the valance in the same fabric as your curtains or choose a coordinating fabric. Left unlined, a valance makes a fresh treatment for a child's bedroom window or cottage-style curtains and sheers. If your curtains are lined, it's quite easy to line the valance too, to give it the same substance as the curtains.

Trimming the valance enhances the simplest window dressing. You can dress an elegant damask with a deep fringe, add a lace frill to a pretty floral or cheerful bobble fringing to plain cottons.

▲ *Made in the same fabric as the curtains, a straight, evenly gathered valance rounds off a stylish window treatment, comprising curtains plus a coordinating blind, with great panache.*

Making an unlined valance

A valance is generally hung on a special valance track that sits in front of the main curtain track. Valance tracks are available from do-it-yourself and department stores. The valance track clips on to an existing curtain track by means of extended brackets, and bends round to return to the wall at each end.

Alternatively, you can mount the valance on a pelmet shelf above the window (see page 75 for putting up a pelmet shelf). To hang the valance, you use a special valance heading tape that has a fuzzy surface. After gathering, this is simply pressed against the hooked side of a strip of Velcro (touch-and-close fastening) that is stapled to the front edge of the pelmet shelf.

(see page 75 for putting up a pelmet shelf)

You will need

- ◆ Furnishing fabric
- ◆ Heading tape – the total ungathered valance width, plus 10cm (4in) (see step 2 below)
- ◆ Valance track and glide hooks
- ◆ Matching thread
- ◆ Tape measure
- ◆ Pins
- ◆ Iron

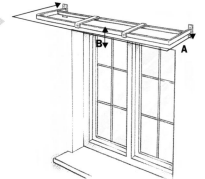

1 Measuring up For the finished valance width, measure the width of the track and add 30cm (12in) for the return to the wall at each end (**A**). For the finished depth, measure from the top of the track to at least 2.5cm (1in) below the top of the glass window panes (**B**). To get the cut length, add 9.5cm (3¾in) for the top turning and hem.

2 Calculating fabric quantities Decide on the heading tape you want to use. Multiply the finished valance width by the heading tape allowance – usually by two but sometimes more. Divide by the fabric width and round up the answer to find out how many widths of fabric you need. Multiply the total widths by the cut length to work out the total length of fabric.

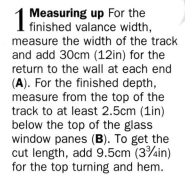

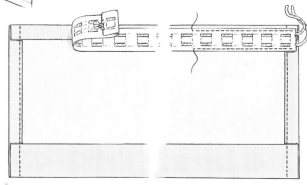

5 Adding the heading tape Turn under 2.5cm (1in) at the top edge and press. Apply the heading tape 6mm (¼in) down from the top fold, neatening each end as in steps **8-11** on page 18, on making unlined curtains.

6 Finishing off Pull up the heading tape cords to the finished width, tie off and finish as in the instructions for making unlined curtains.

3 Cutting and joining widths Straighten the raw edge of the fabric. Cut out the required number of cut lengths. Right sides together, pin and then stitch short ends together to form one long strip. With an uneven number of widths, divide one width in half and join one half at each end. Press the seams open.

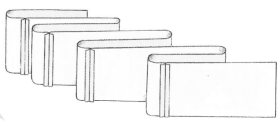

7 Hanging the valance Fix the valance track in place following the instructions on the pack. Arrange the gathers of the valance evenly and slip the glide hooks into the tape at 10cm (4in) intervals. Then clip the glide hooks over the valance track.

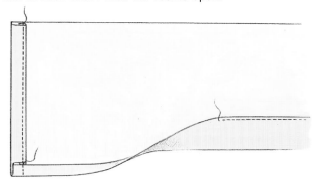

4 Hemming the sides and base To neaten the side edges, press under 1cm (³⁄₈in) and then 2cm (¾in). Pin and stitch, using matching thread. Along the lower edge, press under 1.5cm (⁵⁄₈in), then 5cm (2in). Pin and stitch along edge close to the fold.

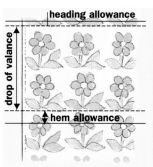

heading allowance

drop of valance

hem allowance

Tip

PATTERN REPEAT
If you are using a fabric with a marked pattern repeat, adjust the drop of the valance to take this into account – allowing for one or two whole repeats to fit exactly between heading and hem.

Making a lined valance

Lining gives the valance more weight, making the folds look fuller. It also eliminates the stitching line along the hem edge, giving a more professional appearance. You need to buy the same amount of lining as fabric.

1 Joining fabric and lining strips Cut the fabric as for an unlined valance. For the lining, cut the same number of widths, but 5cm (2in) shorter than the fabric. Join the fabric widths together, as in *step 3, Making an unlined valance,* and join the lining widths in the same way.

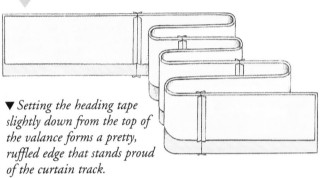

▼ *Setting the heading tape slightly down from the top of the valance forms a pretty, ruffled edge that stands proud of the curtain track.*

2 Attaching the lining Mark the centre of the fabric and lining strips on the lower edges. Pin the lower edges together, right sides together, matching centre points. Stitch a 1.5cm (⅝in) seam, then press the seam open. Trim off any extra lining at the ends to align with fabric.

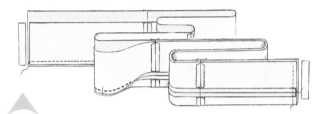

3 Neatening the lining With right sides together, bring the two top edges together so the bottom seam is brought up the back of the valance. Pin and stitch the sides together, taking a 1.5cm (⅝in) seam allowance. Turn out to the right side and press.

4 Finishing and hanging Complete and hang the valance as in *steps 5-7, Making an unlined valance,* treating the two layers of fabric and lining as one.

Trimming a valance

To add designer style, finish off the valance with a trimming. Here the trimming is stitched to the front of the valance, so you need either a flat braid or a fringing with an attractive heading. Buy enough for the full, ungathered width of the valance, plus 5cm (2in).

Use the machine method for flat braids or fringing, which feeds easily under the machine foot. Stitch bulky, textured braids on by hand. You add the trim before applying the heading tape.

To neaten the trimming, turn under 1cm (⅜in) at the beginning and the same again at the end. When sewing on the trimming, be careful to keep it lying slack on the fabric. If it is tight, the fabric puckers underneath as you sew.

▼ *Trimming the edge of the valance with a plain fringing defines the lines of the window treatment and adds a professional edge. The trim need not be expensive for effective results.*

UNWINDING **Tip**
If the trim has been wound tightly on a card, unwind it and leave it lying loose overnight before sewing it on to give it time to relax.

Machine stitching method

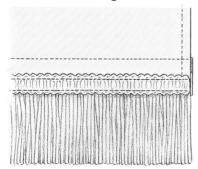

Attaching flat trim Pin trim to valance hem, inserting pins at right angles, leaving any fringe hanging below. Machine stitch close to each edge of trim, stitching over pins before removing to avoid trim edging forward.

Handstitching method

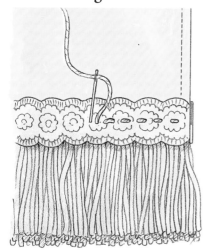

Attaching trim by hand Position trim on valance hem, with fringe hanging below valance. Use a matching thread and small running stitches to attach trim. For wide braid or fringing with a deep heading, work two rows of stab stitching, close to each edge.

Shaped curtain valances

*A shaped curtain valance adds that made-to-measure
look, and makes a graceful, elegant frame for the window. Emphasize
the pretty shape with trimming to complete the effect.*

A curtain valance with a shaped hem makes a useful alternative to the simpler straight version. It adds interest and movement to the curtain treatment – drawing attention to a beautiful texture or pattern – and makes the most of the height of the room, as your eye follows the curve up.

You can tailor the shape to suit the window, so that the valance is longer at the sides, where it hangs in front of the curtains, but shorter in the middle to let in maximum light. Choose the shape to suit the room – an undulating curve suits many florals, while a Gothic arch adds a dramatic touch.

Unless you are adding a frill or a deep fringe, it is wise to line the valance with contrasting fabric, as the reverse side may peep out as the bottom edge rises and falls. You can make a feature of this by picking out a strong, plain colour from the main fabric, or by using a small pattern in a toning colour. Trimmings – such as narrow frills, braid, binding or rich fringing – define the shape well and can be carefully chosen to link in with the colour scheme of the room.

◀ *The valance can be made
with the heading of your
choice – from a simple casing
slotted on to a rod, as shown
here, to one formed by a
heading tape or by hand.*

Making a shaped valance

Decide on the shape and depth of the valance before you start, using the usual proportions of about a sixth of the total curtain length to calculate the depth. Work out the fabric quantities according to the fullness required for the heading tape: twice the finished width for standard gathering tape, two and a half times for pencil pleating, and so on, and remember to include the returns in your calculations.

Fixtures and fittings

See page 56 for information on valance tracks, which are fitted to the front of a standard track, and page 75 on fitting a pelmet shelf. Fix the valance track or pelmet shelf before taking any measurements.

You will need

- ◆ **Furnishing and lining fabric**
- ◆ **Heading tape**
- ◆ **Valance track and glide hooks**
- ◆ **Matching thread**
- ◆ **Tape measure and pencil**
- ◆ **Brown paper for template and newspaper for pattern**

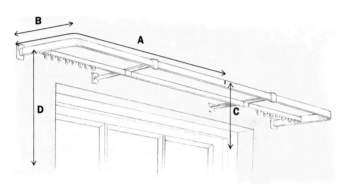

1 Measuring up Mark the centre point of the valance track with a pencil. Measure from this point along the track to the wall at one side (**A**), including the return (**B**). Measure the shortest required depth (**C**), and the longest required depth (**D**).

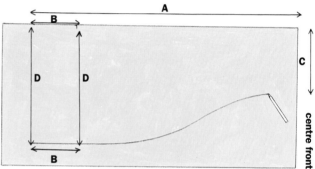

2 Making the half-template Using the measurements from step **1**, draw the finished size of the valance on brown paper, marking in the shortest depth **C** and the longest depth **D**, as shown. Mark in the return **B** at the top and lower edge, then draw in the curve between lower **B** and **C**.

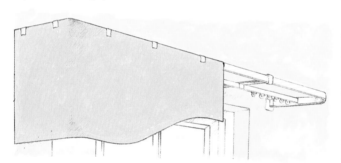

3 Checking the effect Stand back to check the shape from a distance. When you are happy with the effect, cut out the template. Use masking tape to fix the template in place on one half of the window. Check the effect again, and trim the template or cut another one if necessary.

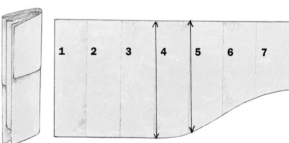

4 Dividing the template Keeping the top edges level, fold the template in half across the width, then fold in half again. Repeat until the sections measure about 15cm (6in) wide. Open out the template and number each fold clearly, including the side edges. Mark in the depth of each fold.

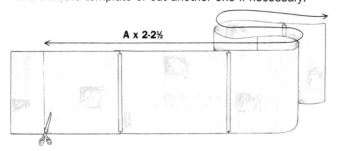

5 Cutting a pattern For the pattern width, multiply the template width by the fullness required for your heading tape (2-2½ times the finished size). Tape together enough sheets of newspaper to make up this measurement, and trim it to the exact width required.

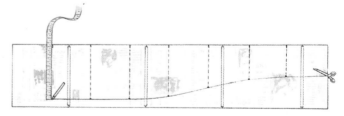

6 Shaping the pattern Fold the pattern into the same number of folds as the template, and number the folds in the same way. Measure the depth of each template fold and mark the same depth on the corresponding fold on the pattern. Join the marks in a sweeping line. Cut out.

◀ *Emphasize the sweeping lines of a simply shaped valance with a subtle or emphatic edging. Here, a piped double frill, made of self-fabric and a plain blue, helps to draw the eye to the elegant curves.*

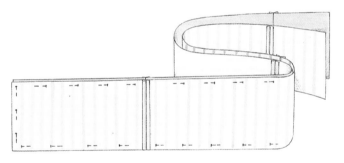

7 Preparing fabric Cut enough widths of fabric and lining to measure **D** plus 4cm (1⅝in) deep, to make a strip twice the width of the pattern, plus a 1.5cm (⅝in) seam allowance at each end. Join widths; press seams open. Right sides together, pin fabric to lining and fold in half widthways.

8 Cutting out Place pattern on fabric with centre front of pattern to fold of fabrics, and its top edge 2.5cm (1in) down from fabric raw edges; pin. Allowing a 1.5cm (⅝in) seam allowance at sides and base, and 2.5cm (1in) at top, cut round the pattern, through both fabric layers.

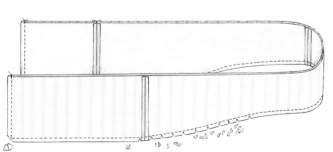

9 Stitching the sides and base Remove the pattern and unfold the fabric. Right sides together, pin and stitch the fabric and lining together at the sides and base. Snip across the seam allowances at the corners and clip into curves along the length. Turn out to right side and press.

10 Completing the valance Follow steps **5-7** on page 56, to complete the valance. Before hanging the valance at the window, lay it out flat with the template on top. Arrange the gathers of the valance to match the shaping of the template.

Valance for a bay window

A gathered valance on a flexible valance track is one of the simplest ways to dress a bay window, but a very wide, straight valance can look monotonous. Shaping the base of the valance, so that it dips and rises, emphasizes the shape of the bay and makes it into a real feature.

For accurate measurements, fix the valance track or pelmet shelf before you start. To achieve a flowing line, it's usual to make the hem dip at the inner corners of the bay and rise over the windows, dropping still lower again at the sides.

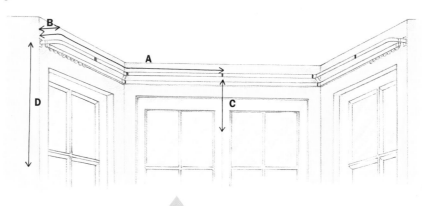

1 Marking the track On the valance track, mark the exact centre of the central window. Mark in each corner point, standing centrally in the angle to line them up exactly. Mark in the centre point of each side window.

2 Measuring up Measure along the track from centre mark to one outer end (**A**), including the return (**B**). Decide on the shortest depth (**C**) and the longest depth (**D**) required, as explained on the previous page.

3 Making a half-template Follow step **2** on the previous page to make up the template, marking in the shortest depth **C** at the centre edge and the longest depth **D** at the outer edge. Don't draw in the curve

4 Marking up the template Mark the corner point by measuring the track from the centre to the corner marks; transfer the measurement to the template. Measure and mark the centre point of the side window.

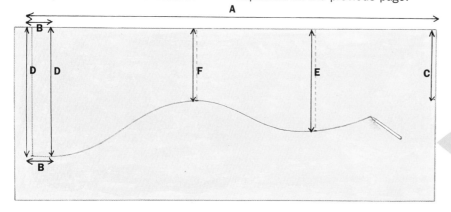

5 Shaping the curves At the corner point, mark the required depth (**E**), which should be somewhere between the shortest and longest depths (**C** and **D**). Mark a shorter depth (**F**) at the side window centre point. Join the marks with sweeping curves. Follow steps **3-10** on the previous pages to make and complete the valance.

The picture (left) shows a valance shaped for a three-sided bay window. Illustrated above are ideas for shaped valances for a five-sided bay (top) and a square bay (above).

Box pleated curtain valance

*With their crisp, orderly appearance, box pleats are
the perfect topping for formal curtains or a cheerful blind.
A flat band ensures a crisp line at the top.*

Box pleated valances have a simple, clean-lined look; the neat folds show a beautiful plain fabric to advantage, especially if you add a border or a subtle row of contrast piping. Stripes or checks make useful guidelines for accurate pleats and provide plenty of scope for imaginative arrangements.

Setting the pleats on a top band helps to get them to hang perfectly and emphasises the design. Fabrics with built-in borders are ideal – you can cut the border off the back edge of the curtains and use it for the top band.

The top band is interlined with heavy interfacing or lightweight buckram, which is sold as heading buckram, in 10-15cm (4-6in) widths. Velcro holds the valance in place on the pelmet shelf.

Box pleats can be closed or open. With closed box pleats, the side edges of the pleats touch, making a very full valance and using lots of fabric – you'll find instructions for making a closed box pleated valance overleaf. Open box pleats, as shown below, are spaced a little apart and use less fabric – instructions for making an open box pleated valance are given on page 66.

▼ *An open box pleated valance adds a hint of formality to a traditional floral window treatment. Piping on the top band, and a slim border at the base of the pleating, underline the elegant theme.*

Valance with closed box pleats

When deciding the depth of the pleats and band, consider the proportions of your window. Most box pleated valances have 10-15cm (4-6in) wide pleats.

For the pleats, you need at least three times the finished width of the valance, including returns, plus 5cm (2in) for turnings and a bit extra for adjusting seams. Allow 7.5cm (3in) extra on the finished depth for the top seam and hem.

For the top band, allow enough for the finished valance width, including the returns, plus 5cm (2in) for turnings, by the finished depth plus 5cm (2in).

Add these two amounts together for the total lining you require.

You will need

◆ Furnishing fabric for pleated section and top band

◆ Contrast fabric and piping cord for piping (optional)

◆ Heavy iron-on interfacing or lightweight buckram

◆ Velcro

◆ Matching thread

◆ Dressmaker's pencils in two different colours

1 Fixing pelmet shelf Following page 75, put up shelf, making sure there is at least 5cm (2in) between front of track and front edge of shelf. Staple Velcro (hard side) along front and side edges of shelf.

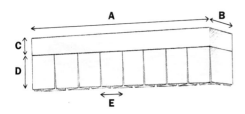

2 Measuring up Measure the front edge of the pelmet shelf (**A**) and the return (**B**). Decide on the depth of the top band (**C**) and the depth of the pleats (**D**). Then decide on the width (**E**) and number of pleats – if possible, this should divide equally into **A** to give a neat finish at the corners.

3 Cutting the top band Cut a piece of buckram measuring twice **B** plus **A**, by **C**. Cut a piece each of fabric and lining to this size, plus 1.5cm (⅝in) all round for seam allowances.

4 Cutting the pleat fabric *For the fabric width:* multiply the buckram width by three and add 3cm (1¼in). *For the depth:* add 5.5cm (2¼in) to **D**. Cut enough full widths of fabric to this depth to make up *at least* the required width – you can trim off any excess later. Tack together to make a long strip. *For the lining:* cut the same number of full widths, but for the depth, add only 5mm (³⁄₈in) to **D**.

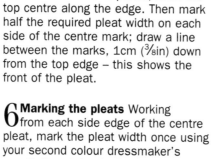

5 Centring the first pleat On the right side of the fabric for the pleated section, and using your first colour dressmaker's pencil, mark the top centre along the edge. Then mark half the required pleat width on each side of the centre mark; draw a line between the marks, 1cm (³⁄₈in) down from the top edge – this shows the front of the pleat.

6 Marking the pleats Working from each side edge of the centre pleat, mark the pleat width once using your second colour dressmaker's pencil, then twice in the first colour; join the last two marks with a line; this marks the front of the next pleat. Continue in this way until you have the required number of pleats, including returns – for accuracy, repeat the measurements along the bottom edge.

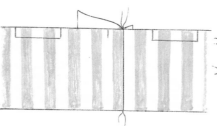

7 Adjusting the seams If a seam crosses the front of a pleat, reposition it so that it will be hidden behind a pleat. Adjust the lining seams in the same way, positioning them adjacent to a fabric seam to avoid excess bulk. Stitch the pleat fabric and lining seams; press open.

8 Lining the pleated section With right sides together and the lower edges level, pin the lining and fabric strips together. Adding 1.5cm (⅝in) seam allowances, trim off the excess from each end of strips; stitch along lower edges. Match the top edges and stitch the side seams; trim corners, turn to the right side and press.

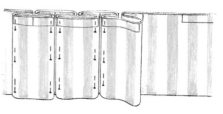

9 Making the pleats Starting at the centre, bring the marks in the first colour at end of each pleat line to the adjacent second colour marks, with the top edges matching; pin. Smooth the pleats down to the bottom edge.

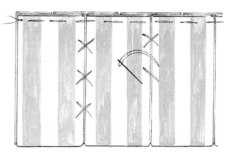

10 Tacking the pleats in place Using double thread, tack along the top edge of the pleats, stitching through all the layers. Make large cross-stitch tacks down the pleats.

11 Preparing the top band If you wish, make up enough contrast piping to fit along the top band and stitch to the lower edge. Cut Velcro (soft side) to fit finished width of valance. Centre it on right side of top band lining, 1.5cm (⅝in) down from top raw edge; stitch all round. With right sides together, stitch band and band lining together along the top edge.

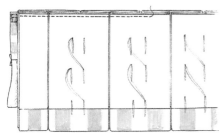

12 **Adding the top band** Right sides together, pin the top band and pleated panel together, sandwiching piping between. The raw side edges of the band should finish 1.5cm (⅝in) beyond the finished side edges of the pleated panel. Stitch through all layers.

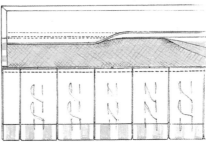

13 **Adding the buckram** Using a warm iron, fuse the buckram to the wrong side of the top band, with the lower edge of the buckram on the seam. Press in all of the seam allowances over the buckram.

▲ *This elegant valance has closed box pleats, 15cm (6in) wide, giving a full and generous look. Note the use of the stripes – horizontal on the top band, and vertical for the pleated section.*

14 **Completing the valance** On the band lining, press in the seam allowances on remaining three sides. Bring the band lining down to cover the buckram tightly. Slipstitch in place at the sides and lower edge. To hang, mark centre of pelmet shelf and top band and press in place from middle outwards. Unpick the cross tacks.

A regularly spaced, dainty checked fabric, such as the one shown here, takes the hard work out of forming neat, accurate pleats.

Open box pleats

You can create interesting design effects with open box pleats, highlighting different parts of a fabric pattern – experiment with different pleat arrangements to find the look you want. For your pleat fabric, allow for two to two and a half times fullness, depending on the size and number of pleats. All the other materials you will need are listed on page 64.

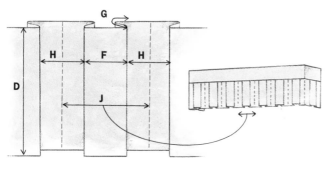

1 Planning the pleats Prepare the pelmet shelf as in step 1 on page 64. Decide pleat depth (**D**). Then decide width of the pleat front (**F**), the back fold (**G**), and the space (**H**). Pleat a strip of paper and measure (**J**), which is the width from centre to centre of **H**. Adjust as necessary, so that **J** divides equally into pelmet shelf width.

2 Cutting the pieces *For the buckram, top band fabric and lining:* follow step **3** on page 64. *To calculate the pleat fabric width:* add **J** to twice **G**, then multiply by the total number of pleats, including pleats on the returns; add 3cm (1¼in) for seams. Then cut the pleat fabric and lining and tack the widths together to make long strips, as in step **4** on page 64.

3 Marking the pleats Using your first colour pencil, follow step **5** on page 64 to centre the first pleat. Working out from the edge of this pleat, use your second colour pencil to measure and mark G then H. Then with the first colour pencil, measure and mark G then F: join G and F with a line to show the front of the next pleat.

4 Adjusting the seams Change back to the second colour pencil and repeat the sequence for the correct number of pleats; for accuracy, repeat along the bottom edge. As in step **7** on page 64, check and reposition the seams in fabric and lining so that they fall within **G**.

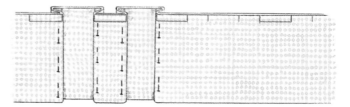

5 Adding the lining and making the pleats Follow steps 7-8 on page 64 to stitch the seams and add the lining. *To make the pleats:* bring the ends of the first colour lines to the adjacent second colour marks, keeping the top and lower edges level; pin in place. Follow steps **10-14** on the previous pages to complete the valance.

Goblet-pleated headings

The king of curtain headings, goblet pleating has a truly regal look – big, bold and sculptural. It makes the perfect finish for an elegant pair of floor-length curtains or a crisply formal valance.

So called because the pleats are shaped like wine goblets, this grand heading gives the simplest of fabrics a special look. They may look complicated to make, but don't worry – a clever, purpose-made heading tape does all the hard work, giving impressive results for very little effort. As the heading itself is 14cm (5½in) deep, its proportions suit longer curtains. Or you can add a flourish to existing, full-length curtains by topping them with a goblet-pleated valance.

Choose mediumweight, firmly woven fabrics, so that the pleats hold their shape and the curtains drape well. Damask, velvet, textured cottons or linen union all work well and play up the formal look; crisp, heavyweight floral chintzes are perfect for an elegant, country house style in sitting rooms or bedrooms.

◀ *Full-length cream curtains, topped with elegant goblet pleats, add a refreshing touch to a bedroom.*

Supporting the curtain

The pleats are supported by double-pronged Tridis hooks, which are available from department stores. You need one hook for each pleat, plus one at each end of the curtain. The tape has three rows of hook pockets. If you insert the hooks in the top row (**A**), the top of the curtain stands 1cm (⅜in) above the eye of the runner or pole ring. The middle row (**B**) gives a 3cm (1¼in) stand-up, and the bottom row (**C**), 5cm (2in). You need to allow for your chosen depth of stand-up when measuring for the finished length of the curtain.

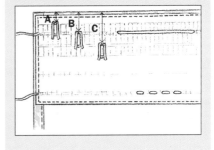

Making goblet-pleated curtains

Goblet-pleated tape pulls up to double fullness, so you need to allow enough fabric to make up twice the width of your pole or track. Buy an extra 25cm (10in) of heading tape per curtain to allow for centring the tape across the curtain width.

The pleat position on the tape is where the upper cord lies on the surface of the tape. The instructions given here show how to apply the heading without the stitching showing along the top front edge of the pleats, giving a professional finish.

1 Measuring up Measure up for the curtains as on pages 13–14. For the finished curtain length, measure from the eye of the runner or ring, add an appropriate amount for the stand-up (see previous page), then add the usual allowances for the cut length.

2 Making up the curtain Cut out and make up the curtains, following pages 17–18, steps **2-7**, for unlined curtains and pages 19–20 for lined. When preparing the heading, press over the top of the fabric as usual, but do not add 1cm (³⁄₈in) at the top.

3 Positioning the heading tape Open out the top fold. Lay the tape right side up, on right side of curtain, so its upper edge (nearest the pockets) lies just above the foldline. Centre the tape across the width, so there is a pleat at least 5cm (2in) from each end of the curtain. Pin in place. Cut the tape off in the middle of the next pleat.

You will need

- ◆ Furnishing fabric
- ◆ Lining fabric (optional)
- ◆ Matching thread
- ◆ Goblet-pleated heading tape
- ◆ Cord tidies (optional)
- ◆ Double-prong (Tridis) curtain hooks
- ◆ Tissue, wadding or cotton wool for padding pleats
- ◆ Tape measure
- ◆ Scissors
- ◆ Pins

▶ *A single full-length curtain, drawn to the side of a wide arch between two rooms, shows an attractive contrast lining to full advantage, while the covered buttons accentuate the sculptured shape of each goblet pleat.*

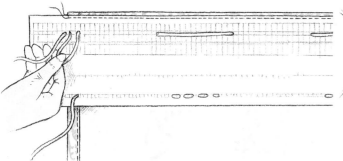

4 Stitching upper edge of tape Stitch along the upper edge of the tape, then turn it to the wrong side of the curtain along the foldline. Pull the cords out 1cm (³⁄₈in) within the side edges of the curtain, then trim the tape ends to overlap the edge of the curtain by 2.5cm (1in).

6 Pulling up the pleats At the leading edge, where the curtains will meet, tie each cord in a firm knot and secure with a few stitches. Pull up the free end of the top cord to position the pleats, then pull the bottom cord to pinch the pleats at the goblet stems. Tie off the cords separately and wind round a cord tidy or into a neat bundle.

5 Stitching lower edge Fold the tape end over the edge of the curtain at each side, between turned-down heading and main curtain. Pin and stitch the remaining three sides of the tape, stitching the lower edge in the same direction as the upper edge and taking care not to catch the cords in the stitching.

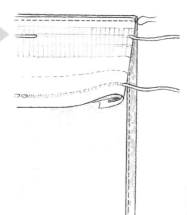

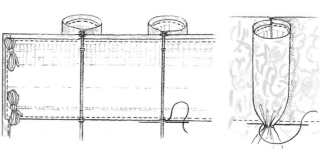

7 Neatening the pleats On the wrong side of the curtain, make a few stitches into the heading tape at the top and bottom of each goblet. On the right side, secure the pinch pleats by making a few stitches across the bottom of each goblet.

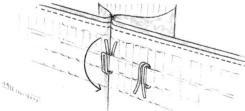

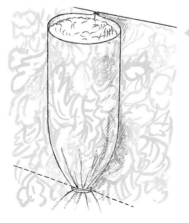

8 Inserting the hooks Ease the prongs of a hook upwards through the adjacent pockets on either side of a pleat, in the row you have chosen. Pull the hook over so that the prongs point downwards. Repeat for the remaining pleats, then insert hooks through adjacent pockets at each end of the curtain tape.

9 Padding out the pleats Make sure that the goblet pleats retain their shape by padding them out with crumpled tissue paper, cotton wool or rolled up wadding, making sure that it does not show at the top of the pleat. Then hang the finished curtain.

Making a goblet-headed valance

The elegant shaping of goblet pleats makes for a very stylish valance, but the proportions are all-important: the finished valance should be at least 35cm (13¾in) deep – 2½ times the pleat depth. You must also centre the pleats across the width of the valance, ideally with a pleat on each corner. The ends are finished last, allowing you to pull up and adjust the pleats to fit the track or pelmet, then cut the valance to size.

You can hang the valance from a valance track or secure it to the front of a pelmet shelf using tacks. Allow enough widths to make a strip twice the length of the track or pelmet shelf.

You will need

- Furnishing fabric
- Lining fabric (optional)
- Matching thread
- Goblet-pleated heading tape
- Cord tidies (optional)
- Double-prong (Tridis) curtain hooks, if hanging from a valance track; or small tacks and a hammer, if securing to a pelmet shelf
- Tissue, wadding or cotton wool for stuffing the pleats
- Tape measure
- Scissors, pins

Make a dramatic statement by topping lined curtains with a valance made in cleverly coordinated fabrics. The self-covered buttons in bright lime green add a stylish finishing touch.

1 Making the strip Measure up, cut out and make up the basic fabric valance, following page 56, steps **1-4**, for an unlined valance and page 57, steps **1-3**, for a lined valance, but do not hem the side edges at this point.

3 Stitching the tape Stitch along upper edge of tape, leaving 5cm (2in) unstitched at each end. Fold tape to wrong side of valance. Stitch along the lower edge, stitching in same direction as before and stopping 5cm (2in) short of sides.

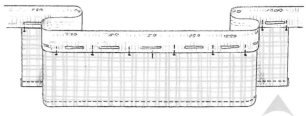

2 Positioning the tape Turn under 2.5cm (1in) at top edge of valance and press. Mark centre of valance, then lay it right side up with top fold opened out. Position tape so its upper edge (nearest to hook pockets) lies just above the foldline, centring a pleat at the centre mark. Pin in place from centre outwards.

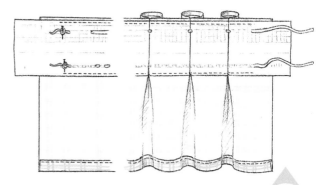

4 Forming the goblet pleats At one side of the valance, pull the cords free, level with the beginning of the stitching. Secure the cords temporarily by winding each end around a pin. At the other end, pull the cords free in the same way, then pull up the pleats, as described in *Making goblet-pleated curtains*, step **6**.

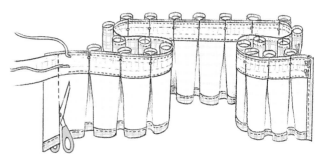

5 Finishing the side edges From the centre pleat, measure half finished valance width and mark. Remove securing pins. Trim the valance and tape 3cm (1¼in) outside the mark. Turn under a double hem at side edges of fabric, then turn the tape under and stitch. Repeat for the other side. Secure and neaten the pleats, as in *Making goblet-pleated curtains*, steps **6-7**.

6 Hanging the valance *For a valance track,* insert the hooks as in *Making goblet-pleated curtains*, step **8**. Push the hooks over the track itself, positioning centre pleat first and working outwards. *For a pelmet shelf,* secure valance with a small tack through back of each pleat, starting with centre pleat. Pad out pleats as before.

Easy pelmets

*For a simple, effective way to frame your window and
hide the curtain track, try a pelmet. Make the most of the special
products available for a professional finish.*

A novel idea is to let the main motifs in a fabric print dictate the shape of the pelmet edge. These dramatic figures, spotlit in white, are ideal for this treatment.

A pelmet is a flat band of fabric fixed to the front of a pelmet shelf, hiding the track and the top of the window. Usually, the pelmet is stiffened with a backing fabric, which ensures that the fabric hangs smoothly. The lower edge can be straight, or cut in a decorative shape. With its simple structure it displays patterned fabric to perfection: alternatively, you can spark up a plain fabric with a striking trim or a contrast band along the base.

Traditionally, pelmets are stiffened with buckram (a heavy interfacing) and padded with interlining or bump. A special, self-adhesive pelmet stiffener is also available, which is more expensive than buckram, but is quicker to use. It has a peel-off backing and is printed with a grid for drawing your own design, or you can choose from a selection of printed shapes. You then stick the fabric directly on to the stiffener, and hide the raw edge with a decorative braid.

Making a buckram pelmet

You need a pelmet shelf to support the pelmet. Instructions for making a pelmet shelf are given on page 75. It is important to fix this before measuring for the pelmet. Aim to make the pelmet deep enough to conceal the top of the window, even at the shallowest point of the shape.

Pelmet buckram comes in a choice of widths; buy the next width up from your finished pelmet depth and make sure that it is fusible on one side.

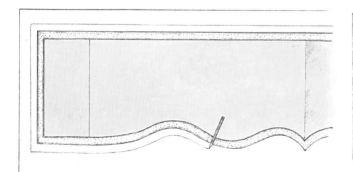

You will need

◆ Furnishing fabric

◆ Matching thread

◆ Heavyweight single-sided fusible buckram

◆ Interlining or lightweight wadding

◆ Fabric for lining

◆ Velcro

◆ Scissors

◆ Needle and pins

◆ Hammer and tacks

▶ *The simple lines of a straight pelmet look just as smart as one with more complicated shaping – and it is the easiest version to make. Here, for a coordinated look, the pelmet, curtains and tiebacks are all made using the same fabric.*

1 Fixing the pelmet shelf Cut the timber, fix the angle brackets and attach the pelmet shelf. If you are planning to make a deep pelmet, or if the window is very wide, add end pieces to the shelf for rigidity as shown above. Then attach the hard side of the Velcro all round the pelmet shelf, including the returns, putting the soft aside for the pelmet.

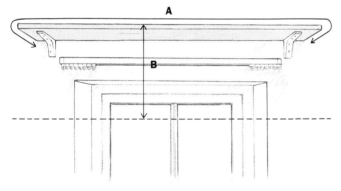

2 Measuring up *For the width:* measure all round the pelmet shelf, from wall to wall (**A**). *For the depth:* measure the finished depth you want (**B**), at the deepest point of the shape, if any.

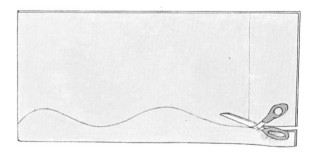

3 Making a pattern Cut paper to measure **A** by **B**. For a shaped pelmet, mark in the returns and fold pattern in half widthways. Draw the shape, working from the fold out to returns. Cut out. Pin pattern to shelf to check the shape.

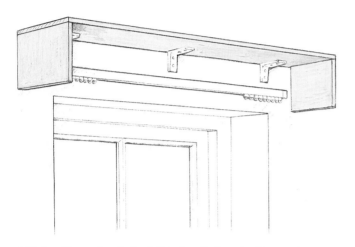

4 Cutting out Draw round the pattern on the buckram and cut it out. Adding 1cm (³⁄₈in) all round, cut it out again in interlining and lining. For the fabric, add 2cm (³⁄₄in) all round the pattern before cutting it out. (Join panels on either side of a width of fabric if necessary.)

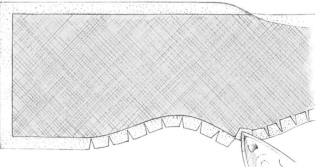

5 Adding the interlining Lay the buckram on the interlining, fusible side up. Clipping and notching where necessary, turn the edge of the interlining up over the buckram on all edges, fusing in place with the tip of the iron. Leave to cool.

6 Adding the fabric Lay the fabric wrong side up, then centre the buckram, interlined side down, on top. Turn up the fabric edges in the same way as for the interlining, and fuse to the buckram with the tip of the iron.

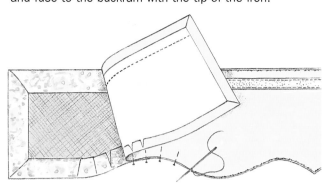

7 Applying the Velcro On the right side of the lining, centre the soft side of the Velcro along the top edge, 1cm (⅜in) down. Pin and stitch all round the Velcro, close to the edges.

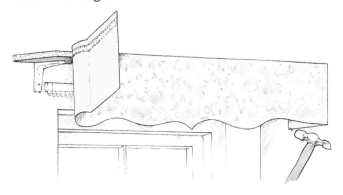

8 Lining the pelmet Clipping and notching where necessary, turn under 1cm (⅜in) all round the lining piece. Lay the lining on the back of the pelmet, pin in place and slipstitch all round. For extra security, fuse the lining to the buckram with a warm iron.

9 Hanging the pelmet Crease the pelmet gently at the corner points to make the returns. Centre the pelmet on the pelmet shelf and press it in place on the Velcro. If necessary, anchor the bottom corners by nailing a small tack through the fabric into the wall.

Making a quick pelmet

There are two types of self-adhesive pelmet stiffener available. **Double-sided stiffener** has peel-off paper on both sides, so that you can add a lining on the back – you need to stitch Velcro on as for the buckram version.

Single-sided stiffener has a special velour finish on the back which will stick to the hard side of the Velcro, so you don't need to use lining or the soft side of the Velcro.

You will need

- Furnishing fabric
- Double-sided or single-sided pelmet stiffener
- Braid
- Lining (for single-sided stiffener)
- Velcro (for single-sided stiffener)
- Scissors
- Tailor's chalk
- Fabric adhesive

▶ *A subtle, Cupid's bow shaped pelmet is trimmed with a jolly bobble fringe. The fringe adds textural interest to the treatment.*

▶ *The undulating curves of this pelmet echo the soft curved shapes of the fruity fabric print. A braid edging, in addition to emphasizing the shape of the pelmet, helps to colour coordinate the total effect.*

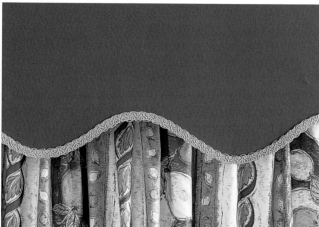

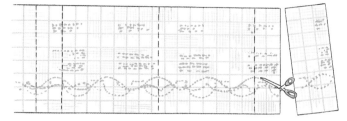

1 Measuring up Fix the pelmet shelf, and measure up, as in steps **1-2** on page 72. Find the centre point of your chosen design on the stiffener, and mark the required width and returns. Cut off the surplus at each end, then cut along the line for your chosen pattern.

2 Preparing fabric Press the fabric and lay it out wrong side up, centring the stiffener over any pattern. Using the chalk, draw round the stiffener. If using lining, draw round the shape in the same way. Stitch on Velcro close to the top chalk line of lining.

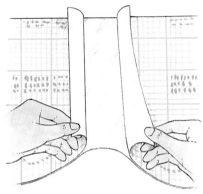

3 Preparing the stiffener Starting at centre of stiffener strip, lift, then cut through centre of the paper covering. Peel it back about 5cm (2in) on each side and carefully position it, sticky side down, on the chalked shape.

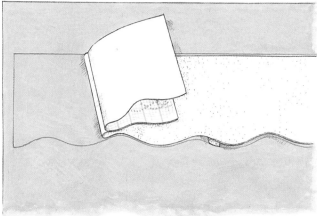

4 Applying the stiffener Making sure there are no wrinkles, smooth the sticky surface on to the fabric, peeling back covering a little at a time. Continue to ends, then trim away all the excess fabric level with edge of stiffener. If necessary, repeat on other side to add lining.

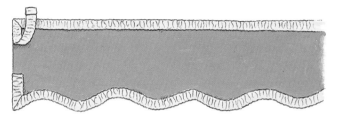

5 Trimming the pelmet Starting on one side edge, glue the braid all round to cover the raw edges, mitring it neatly at the corners and overlapping it at the join. Finally, hang the pelmet, as in step **9** on the previous page.

Pelmets step-by-step

A pelmet gives a professional finish to the top of curtains. It conceals the curtain track and heading and helps to balance the proportions of a window.

Alternatively, you can attach a frilled or pleated valance. A valance is gathered up in the same way as a curtain, using curtain heading tape, and it is hung from a curtain track or special stick-on tape.

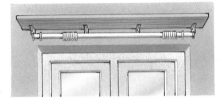

Pelmet shelf This is a plywood shelf, usually about 10cm (4in) deep, with a fabric front. Pelmet shelves suit most types of window, but for very wide windows a pelmet box is more suitable (see right).

You can attach a stiffened fabric pelmet to the front of the shelf using touch-and-close fastening or screw eyes. The pelmet can have a straight lower edge, or it can be shaped for a more decorative finish.

Pelmet box This is a pelmet shelf with square or rectangular end pieces. Pelmet boxes can have a stiffened fabric front, like pelmet shelves, or a wooden front. Wooden fronts can be painted and decorated in the same way as other interior woodwork, or they can be covered with wallpaper.

Kit pelmets These can be used to hang pelmets or valances on most types of window, and they are the easiest option for bay or bow windows as they can be bent or shaped to fit awkward angles. Pelmet kits include a strip of white-finished PVC which clips on to metal brackets. You don't have to drill into the wall and there are special clip-on sections for finishing the ends. Kits are sold in 1.5m (5ft), 2m (6½ft) and 2.6m (8½ft) standard lengths which you cut to fit your windows.

Kit pelmets can be decorated in the same way as wooden-fronted pelmet boxes (see left).

Making a pelmet shelf

You will need

- ◆ **Length of 9mm (⅜in) plywood for the shelf**
- ◆ **3.8cm (1½in) steel angle brackets**
- ◆ **1cm (⅜in) chipboard screws**
- ◆ **3.2cm (1¼in) No.8 woodscrews with wallplugs**
- ◆ **Panel saw**
- ◆ **Jigsaw or surform**
- ◆ **Electric drill and bits**
- ◆ **Hammer and screwdriver**
- ◆ **Try square**
- ◆ **Sandpaper**
- ◆ **Metal tape**
- ◆ **Vice**

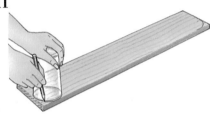

1 Measuring up Decide how far you want the pelmet to extend beyond the curtain track at each end – most pelmet shelves extend by at least 5cm (2in) on each side. Double this measure and add it to the length of the track. This will be the length of your pelmet shelf. The pelmet should be deep enough to cover the track and curtain heading: 10-15cm (4-6in) is usually enough.

2 Making the shelf Mark the width and length of the shelf on the plywood and cut it. To soften the line of the pelmet, draw round a glass at each of the two front corners. Fix the shelf in a vice or clamp. Using a jigsaw or a surform tool, round off the corners along the marked lines.

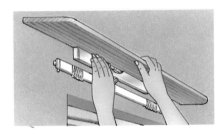

3 Marking the position Position the shelf centrally, just above the curtain track and/or window frame. Use a carpenter's level to check that it is horizontal, then mark the position with a pencil.

4 Fixing up the shelf Fix the pelmet in place with the angle brackets, spacing them at 30cm (1ft) intervals.

If there isn't enough space above the window for the fixings, screw the shelf brackets to the outer edges of the window frame.

Making a pelmet box

Measure and cut a pelmet shelf as for *Making a pelmet shelf*, steps **1** and **2**, but don't round off the corners. Cut the sides to fit the shelf – for example, for a 10cm (4in) deep shelf cut the side pieces 10cm (4in) square.

Fix the top and sides together with wood glue and screws, making sure the screw heads are sunk below the surface. Use a try square to keep the corners at right angles. Leave the glue to dry, then sand any rough edges.

Fix the pelmet box in position as for *Making a pelmet shelf*, step **3**.

Making a fabric pelmet

Fabric pelmets were traditionally stiffened with buckram, a rigid, woven fabric, and interlined with domette. This method is time-consuming, so instead, follow the steps to make an easy fabric pelmet using self-adhesive stiffener. Pelmet styles are printed on the backing sheet – you can use one of these or create your own.

You will need

- ◆ **Wallpaper or stiff paper for a template (optional)**
- ◆ **Pelmet fabric**
- ◆ **Lining fabric**
- ◆ **Double-sided self-adhesive stiffener**
- ◆ **Sewing thread and pins**
- ◆ **Scissors**
- ◆ **Tape measure**
- ◆ **Touch-and-close fastening, such as Velcro**
- ◆ **Adhesive**
- ◆ **Braid trim (optional)**

Making a template

If you want your fabric pelmet to have a decorative edge, follow steps **1-3**. If you want it to have a straight edge, omit steps **2-3**.

1 Measuring up Measure the front of the pelmet shelf, and around the side edges if you're using a pelmet box. If you are making a straight-edged pelmet, cut a strip of paper this length by the depth of the finished pelmet – most pelmets are 15-30cm (6-12in) deep. If you're making a decorative pelmet, cut the paper slightly wider than the deepest section of the planned shape.

NO-SEW PELMET
You can make a simple pelmet without sewing a single stitch using single-sided fabric stiffener. Just cut the fabric 2cm (¾in) larger all round than the finished size of the pelmet. Cut the stiffener to shape, peel off the backing and stick it to the wrong side of the fabric. Then trim the fabric edges flush with the stiffener.

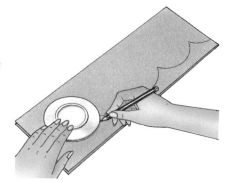

2 Drawing the template Fold the paper in half widthways, creasing it at the centre. Measure and mark the corner positions if any, then crease them.

Draw the intended shape on the paper, working from the centre out to one of the corners. Measure accurately to make sure that repeated shapes are the same size.

3 Cutting the template With the paper still folded, cut out the shape along the marked line through both the layers to ensure it's symmetrical. Trim the template to the finished size of the pelmet.

Making the pelmet

1 Cutting the fabric If you're using a template, cut a piece of the main fabric and a piece of lining fabric 2.5cm (1in) larger than the pelmet template all round. Cut a piece of the self-adhesive pelmet stiffener to the finished shape and size of the pelmet.

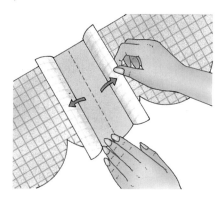

2 Adding the stiffener Ease the backing paper from the centre of the stiffener, cut it across the width and peel back a little on each side. Place the main fabric centrally on top, right side up, and press it down. Continue peeling away the backing paper while smoothing the fabric.

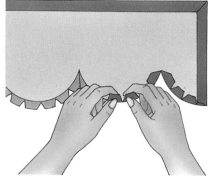

3 Neatening the edges Clip into the fabric seam allowance around the curves and at the corners, and press the allowances to the wrong side of the pelmet. Peel the backing off the other side of the stiffener and press down the fabric turnings to stick them.

4 Preparing the lining material Press a 1.5cm (⅝in) turning to the wrong side of the lining all round. Sew the soft part of the touch-and-close fastening to the right side of the lining, along the top edge.

5 Attaching the lining With the wrong side of the lining to the wrong side of pelmet, smooth the lining down on to the adhesive surface, working from the centre outwards. Then slipstitch it to the main fabric all round.

6 Finishing the pelmet If you like, glue or slipstitch a decorative braid trim to the top and/or bottom of the pelmet, folding the braid into neat mitres at the corners.

Glue the hooked half of the touch-and-close fastening to the front edge of the pelmet shelf, then press the pelmet in place.

Festoon pelmet

*This softly draped festoon pelmet gives a window
grace and style, enhancing an elegant fabric and making
the most of the window height.*

A festoon pelmet hangs across the top of the window in a series of looping swags, or festoons. The fabric is ruched up between each swag to form soft ruffles, and interesting trimmings turn the window feature into a true design statement. The festoon pelmet featured here has a dainty fan-edge trim along the bottom edge to enhance the flowing lines. The shape is also beautifully highlighted at the top by rope, looped and twisted to form elaborate open knots which resemble three-lobed clover leaves.

The pelmet is made from a single straight strip of fabric, with tiny tucks at the top of each ruching line to give a little fullness. Festoon tape, stitched down the pelmet at regular intervals, has built-in gathering cords which make fast work of the ruching. The pelmet is fixed on to a pelmet shelf with Velcro.

▼ *A festoon pelmet tops a window with real style, creating a frame of patterned fabric. It is fixed to a pelmet shelf which is completely concealed by the fabric.*

Making a festoon pelmet

You should cut the pelmet to twice the finished depth, to allow for the ruching, plus seam allowances. Make each festoon about 30-40cm (12-16in) wide – a standard window will have three or four festoons with four or five ruching lines on the front, plus one more festoon at each side edge. Decide how many festoons you need before buying the fabric, and remember to allow enough extra fabric to reach round the sides.

You will need

- ◆ **Furnishing fabric**
- ◆ **Festoon blind tape**
- ◆ **Velcro**
- ◆ **Trimming (optional)**
- ◆ **Rope (optional)**
- ◆ **Tape measure**
- ◆ **Scissors**
- ◆ **Pins**
- ◆ **Dressmaker's pencil**

Fixing the pelmet

Fix the pelmet shelf in place before measuring up. The front edge of the pelmet needs to extend 5cm (2in) in front of the track, so that you can draw the curtains without disturbing the swags.

If your curtain track is not yet in place, use a 10cm (4in) deep pelmet shelf. Fix the track to the underside and 5cm (2in) in from the outside edge of the shelf. If your curtain track is already fixed to the wall, your pelmet shelf should be a minimum of 5cm (2in) deep.

Staple the hard side of the Velcro to the front and side edges of the pelmet shelf.

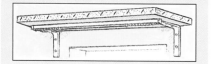

1 Measuring up *For the finished depth:* measure the depth from the top of the pelmet shelf (**A**). *For the width:* measure round the sides and front of the pelmet shelf (**B**).

2 Cutting out the fabric For the cut depth, double the finished depth **A** and add 8cm (3⅛in). For the total width, add 6cm (2¼in) to **B** for side hems, then add 5cm (2in) for each ruching line. Cut enough strips across the width of the fabric to make up a strip to these measurements.

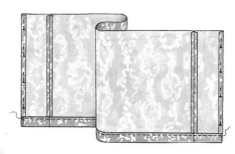

3 Joining and hemming Join all the strips right sides together to make a long strip, and press the seams open. At the side edges, turn under 1cm (⅜in), then 2cm (¾in). Pin the side hems but do not stitch them. At the bottom hem edge, turn under 1cm (⅜in), then 5cm (2in) and stitch.

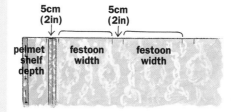

4 Marking the tucks Starting at one end of the strip, on the wrong side of the fabric, measure the pelmet shelf depth (the return), along the top and mark with the dressmaker's pencil. Then measure and mark in the tucks as follows: mark the first 5cm (2in) tuck width, then the festoon width, and then another tuck width. Repeat for each festoon, leaving the return at the other end.

5 Marking the ruching lines At the centre of each tuck allowance, mark a vertical line to 1cm (⅜in) above the bottom edge.

6 Positioning the tapes Pull out the cords at one end of the festoon tape and knot on the wrong side, then turn under 1cm (⅜in) of the tape over the knot. Pin the tape up the first line, cutting it off level with the top. Repeat for each marked line; add another tape on each side hem.

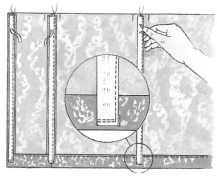

7 Stitching the festoon tape Stitch down one side of each tape, avoiding the cords, and across the bottom; on side hems, stitch on side nearest folded edge. Pull out cords on each tape, 6cm (2¼in) below top edge.

8 Making the tucks On the right side, crease the fabric at each tuck mark, bring the crease to the centre line and pin to 6cm (2¼in) from the top. Tack the tucks in place.

9 **Adding the Velcro** Cut a piece of Velcro (soft side) to length of **B** (see step **1**). Lay it right side up across top edge of pelmet, with its lower edge 2cm (¾in) from the raw edge. Stitch lower edge of the Velcro – take care not to catch the cord ends. Turn to the wrong side, and stitch the other three sides.

10 **Completing the pelmet** Pull up the cords to the required length and knot temporarily. Hang in position and check that all the festoons are the same depth; tie off cords securely, and dress the folds in evenly. You may need to secure the bottom corners to the wall with small tacks.

▲ *Grand and imposing, these matching window treatments make an elegant statement. The rich blue damask contrasts strongly with the yellow walls, while a deep fringe and decorative rope pick out the colour of the pattern.*

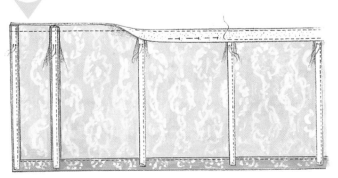

Trimming the festoon pelmet

Scrumptious trimmings can make the most economical fabrics look really luxurious, and create a real design statement. You can also use your trims to link the pelmet to other elements of the colour scheme elsewhere in the room. You can trim the edge with a fan edge or a cut fringe, and for a formal look add a rope trim as explained in the step-by-step instructions below.

Trimming the lower edge

Apply the trimming to the lower edge after you have stitched on the festoon tape, but before pulling up the cords. You will need enough trimming to fit along the total width of the valance, including the returns, plus 5cm (2in) for neatening the ends. For details see step **2** on page 78. To add the trim, refer to page 58.

Adding the looped rope

Choose a firm rope or furnishing cord about 12mm (½in) thick. Check the rope against the fabric and the wall. The colour should show up well against both, as the looped knots stand up above the pelmet shelf.

To work out how much rope you will need, take measurement **B** (refer to step **1** on page 78), and add about 50cm (20in) for each looped knot, plus an extra 10-15cm (4-6in) for the slack between each knot.

Before adding the rope trim, position the pelmet on the pelmet shelf and secure it with pins or a few temporary stitches. When you are happy with the effect, take the pelmet down and stitch the rope in place securely.

1 Securing the end Bind the end of the rope with matching thread and secure the thread with a few stitches. Stitch the end of the rope on the back of the pelmet about halfway down. Then loop the rope gently up to the front corner, and secure with a few stitches.

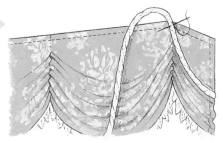

2 Making the looped knot Make a backward loop with rope so that it stands about 5cm (2in) above pelmet. Pin or secure with a few stitches. Continue curve to the left with a similar loop, bringing long end out from behind, and secure again; take rope across and curl it back on top in a figure of eight to complete. Stitch to secure.

3 Completing the rope decoration Allow the rope to fall in a gentle curve across the pelmet, following the drape of the festoon, to the top of the next ruching line. Repeat step **2** to make another looped knot. Continue in this way to the other corner, and finish the return in the same way as at the beginning (see step **1**).

> **LINING THE FESTOON PELMET**
> **Tip**
> Lining always improves the hang of draped fabrics. Cut the lining as the fabric but less 5cm (2in) in depth. Join the lining and main fabric right sides together at their lower edges, then match top raw edges and seam sides before turning to right side. Continue as described for *Making a festoon pelmet*, treating them as one layer.

▶ *Choose a contrasting colour for the rope which will show up well against both the fabric and the wall. On a plain fabric, a rope with two or more colours would work well, but keep to plainer designs to pick out the colour in a patterned fabric.*

Upholstered pelmets

*For a really professional looking, sturdy pelmet, use a
panel of wood as a base and staple fabric on top. It's a surprisingly
quick method and looks impressively substantial.*

Using a board as the base for a pelmet gives you an alternative construction method to the one used for the buckram pelmets, described on pages 71–74. It is very useful if you want to make an especially wide or deep pelmet, when even the heaviest buckram is inclined to buckle and bend. If the pelmet you are making is completely straight, you can even get the base board cut exactly to size.

A straight pelmet can be a very stylish way of complementing a modern room. Try using a fabric with vertical stripes, and cutting a border along the stripes to make a chic contrasting edge; or scatter a plain fabric, backed with wadding, with decorative studs before applying it to the board.

Plywood is quite easy to cut with a panel saw so, if you wish, you can shape the base of the pelmet in undulating

▲ *The crisp, clean lines of the flat pelmets above the window frame and, unusually, the bed, are softened by the scrolling shape at the base edge, delicately picked out with narrow piping.*

curves to flatter your room. Avoid tight curves and sharp corners, as cutting them smoothly, and covering them with fabric, can be difficult. A staple gun makes fast work of applying the layers.

Making an upholstered pelmet

These instructions show you how to make a pelmet with a stitched lower edge. With this method you can add piping or a flanged cord for a contrasting detail. The trimming and lining are machine stitched to the fabric along the lower edge, then wrapped around the board and stapled in place at the top. As the lining comes to the edge of the pelmet, you may wish to choose a coloured lining to match the fabric.

The pelmet is fixed to a pelmet shelf. The base is wrapped in wadding for a padded look, but you could use bump or thin foam sheeting instead. Flexible hinges for the corners – where the pelmet returns to the wall – are made by gluing on calico strips.

Plywood is available from most do-it-yourself stores; it is usually possible to buy half a sheet, cut lengthways. Use 8mm (5⁄16in) staples and 2 ply board for small, light pelmets; for large or heavy pelmets use 10mm (3⁄8in) staples on 3 ply board.

You will need

- ◆ Furnishing fabric and lining fabric
- ◆ Wadding
- ◆ Piping fabric and cord
- ◆ Matching thread
- ◆ Scraps of calico or strong cotton
- ◆ Velcro
- ◆ PVA adhesive
- ◆ 2 or 3 ply board
- ◆ Staples and staple gun
- ◆ Panel saw and sandpaper
- ◆ Hammer and tacks

▶ *A striking floral fabric is displayed to perfection on a matched pair of simple upholstered pelmets. The lower edges are formed into a gently arching line. A simple shape like this is easy to cut and cover with fabric.*

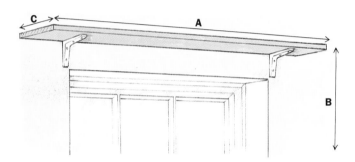

1 Measuring up and cutting out With the pelmet shelf in position, measure the width (**A**) and the depth at the lowest point of shape (**B**). Measure the return (**C**). *For main pelmet:* cut a piece of plywood to measure **A** plus twice the thickness of the ply, by **B**. *For returns:* cut two pieces measuring **C** by **B**.

2 Shaping the board Cut a piece of paper the same size as the main pelmet; fold it in half across the width and draw the required shape along one long edge. Cut out, then draw round it on to the plywood. Cut out with a panel saw, and smooth any rough edges with sandpaper.

3 Making the hinges Cut four pieces of calico 10cm (4in) wide by **B** deep. On front of pelmet, apply a 5cm (2in) strip of adhesive at each end; lay a strip of calico on the adhesive, overlapping each edge by 5cm (2in).

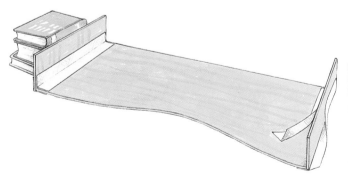

4 Adding returns Apply adhesive to ends of return sections in same way. Then, with main pelmet wrong side up, set returns at right angles to ends and smooth up calico flaps on to glue. Wedge in place. Stick the two remaining calico pieces on the inside of each bend. Leave to dry.

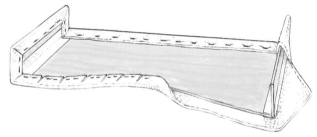

5 Padding the pelmet Cut a piece of wadding 5cm (2in) bigger all round than whole pelmet, including returns. Centre pelmet wrong side up on wadding, and fold excess wadding to inside, stapling first at centre top and working outwards. Trim and clip to fit round curves at lower edge.

6 Cutting the fabric Cut a piece of fabric and lining same size as wadding in step **5**. Lay fabric and lining wrong sides together; centre pelmet pattern on top and pin. Draw around shape, continuing in a straight line along the returns. Trim *lower* edge to within 1.5cm (5⁄8in) of the pencilled line.

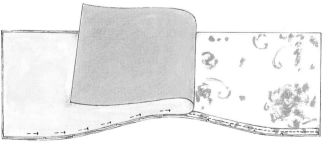

7 Adding piping and lining Make up enough piping to go along lower edge. Apply it along pencilled line on right side of fabric, clipping seam allowances where necessary. Lay fabric and lining right sides together, matching shape, and pin at lower edge. Stitch, sandwiching piping between.

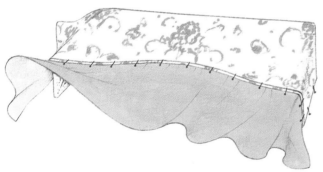

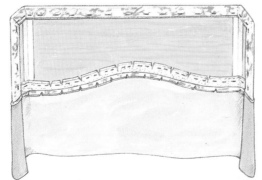

8 Positioning the fabric Place the fabric on the pelmet with the piping following bottom edge exactly. Push pins into wadding to hold the fabric at lower and side edges, smoothing it firmly towards the top and sides.

9 Securing fabric Pull up the fabric over the top edge, stapling 2.5cm (1in) down from the top at 5cm (2in) intervals. Repeat at side edges, forming neat mitres at the corners. Staple again between first row of staples, keeping the tension even and the piping in position.

10 Adding lining and Velcro Smooth lining firmly up to the top. Turn in top edge of lining 1cm (³⁄₈in) below pelmet top and staple in place; continue down sides. Cut a piece of Velcro to go all round top edge of pelmet. Staple soft part on inside of pelmet, level with top edge. Staple hard part around front edge of pelmet shelf.

11 Hanging the pelmet Mark centre of pelmet and shelf. Matching centres, fix pelmet in place, easing returns out, away from the Velcro; then smooth returns into place. Add small tacks on inside bottom corners of returns, as in step **9** on page 73, to secure them to the wall.

Tip

CENTRING A PATTERN
If the fabric you've chosen for the pelmet has an intricate pattern, position it carefully on the pelmet. Cut your pattern from tissue or tracing paper (see step 2), so that you can see the design through it when you cut out the fabric.

Pelmet with stapled lower edge

This no-sew pelmet is a simpler version of the basic upholstered pelmet, shown on the previous pages. It combines a simple technique with a professional finish – and you won't need to sew a single stitch by hand or machine.

The piping or cording is omitted from the lower edge, which means that you can simply staple the fabric on to the pelmet all the way round – if you still want to trim the lower edge, you can glue on braid or fringing after you have finished stapling the wadding, fabric and lining in place.

When you are designing your pelmet, it's important to keep the shape as simple as possible, as you will have to fold the fabric neatly around it. You will need all the same materials as listed on the previous page, except for the piping fabric and cord.

The plump curves of the fruity fabric used on the pelmet are echoed in the generous scoops of the pelmet shaping.

1 Preparing the pelmet Fix the pelmet shelf in position above the window. Then follow steps **1-5** on page 82 to cut out and make up the pelmet board, complete with its hinges and returns, and to cover it with wadding. Then use the paper pattern to cut out the fabric and lining, allowing an extra 5cm (2in) all round for turnings.

2 Applying the fabric Centre the fabric on the pelmet, smoothing it taut over the wadding in both directions, and pushing pins into the wadding all round the pelmet to hold the fabric securely in place. Pull the fabric firmly over the top and sides, securing all round with a few staples.

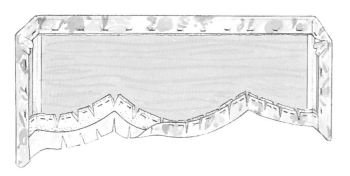

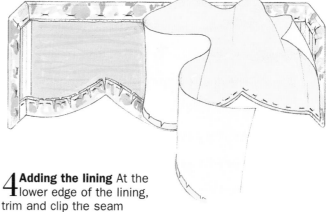

3 Stapling the fabric Clipping into edges of the fabric carefully where necessary, pull the fabric to the wrong side and staple it in place along the shaped edge, keeping the staples well away from the edge. Repeat for the remaining three sides, gently pulling the fabric taut.

4 Adding the lining At the lower edge of the lining, trim and clip the seam allowance to 1cm (³⁄₈in) and press it under. Position on wrong side of pelmet, right side up, and staple neatly in place to cover the raw edges of the fabric. Follow steps **10-11** on the previous page to complete the sides and top edges, add the Velcro and hang the pelmet.

Pennant pelmets

Give your window a sharply stylish edge with a pelmet featuring
deep, zigzag points. Make it plain and simple, elegantly trimmed,
or circus bright with bells on – it's a very flexible design.

The sharp zigzag silhouette of a pennant pelmet adds a smart, distinctive look to any window, and blends well with both period style rooms and contemporary interiors. Use it for a formal pelmet in a traditional design, crisply backed with firm buckram, and accentuate the shape with a decorative braid or contrast binding; or provide a subtle touch of detail for a simple, modern room with a sharply cut, soft pelmet slotted on to a pole.

Draw attention to the points with detailed trimming – tiny tassels, beads or pompons all add character. For a child's room you could create a fun look with gleaming bells to coordinate with a clown theme. For a shipshape boating

▲ *An elegantly dressed bay window is enhanced by deep pennant points. A picot braid delicately emphasizes the shaped edges and the honeycomb fabric motifs.*

theme, cut separate, alternating navy and white pennants. Or make gingham or striped pelmets in a jaunty zigzag shape to top kitchen blinds.

Making a pennant pelmet

These instructions are for a soft pelmet slotted on to a 12mm (½in) rod. To hang a curtain beneath the pelmet, fix a curtain track to the wall behind the rod. For a thicker pole, measure the diameter carefully and add extra for ease in step **5**.

The pelmet is reversible: you can use the same fabric for the front and back, or pick two different fabrics and ring the changes to suit the season. Alternatively, choose a toning lining to complement the main fabric.

Fit the rod above the window before measuring up for the pelmet, positioning it no more than 10cm (4in) above the top of the window recess, otherwise the top of the zigzags may reveal the frame or wall. If you are unsure about the design, draw the shape roughly on paper and hold it up at the window to check the proportions and to see how it looks.

You will need

- ◆ **Furnishing fabric for front**
- ◆ **Lining fabric for back**
- ◆ **Matching thread**
- ◆ **Paper for pattern**
- ◆ **Pencil and ruler**
- ◆ **Dressmaker's pencil**
- ◆ **Knitting or darning needle**

▶ *Add a simple slotted pelmet on a pole to offset cool linen curtains. The pennant shape has a zippy modern look and enhances a neatly coordinating beige and white stripe.*

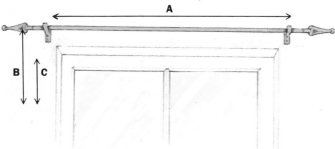

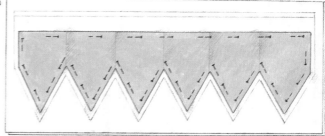

1 Measuring up for the pelmet Decide on the finished width (**A**) and depth (**B**) of the pelmet, measuring from the top of the rod for the latter. Next decide on the depth of the zigzags (**C**), so that the top point of the shape is 2.5-5cm (1-2in) below the glass at the top of the window.

2 Starting the pattern Cut a piece of paper measuring **A** times **B** for the basic pelmet pattern. Then divide the pattern into equal sections, each section being the width of one pennant shape.

3 Making the pennant template Cut a separate piece of paper to the size of one section, as measured in step **2** above, and fold it in half, vertically. On the unfolded side edge of the rectangle, measure up from the bottom corner and mark the depth of the zigzag **C**. Draw a line from this point to the bottom of the fold, as shown. Cut along line, through both layers, and open out.

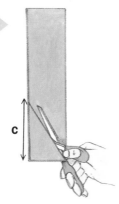

5 Cutting out the fabric With the fabric and lining right sides together, pin the pattern on top. At the top edge, add 2-4cm (¾-1½in) for ease round the rod, then add 1.5cm (⅝in) all round, including the top edge, measuring carefully on the angled edges. Cut out.

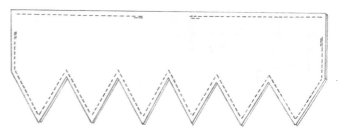

6 Sewing together At each side edge, measure down from the top seamline the depth of the pole plus the ease allowed in step **5**, and mark. Stitch the side and lower edge, starting and stopping at the marks, and pivoting the fabric at the points. Stitch the top edge, starting and stopping 1.5cm (⅝in) from the side edges and leaving a 15cm (6in) opening for turning to right side.

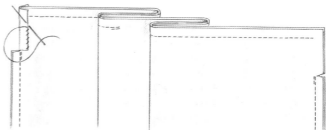

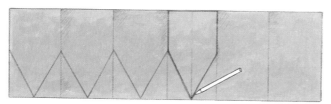

4 Shaping the pattern Place the pennant template over the first section on the paper pattern and draw round the pennant shape. Repeat with all the sections. Cut out.

7 Neatening the side openings Clip the seam allowances to the stitching at the bottom of the side openings. Turn back the seam allowances and slipstitch neatly in place.

8 Trimming the seams Use sharp scissors to trim the other seam allowances to 6mm (¼in). At the zigzag points, snip across each point just below the stitching, then clip the corners again to reduce any unnecessary bulk. At the inner corners of the zigzag points, clip into the seam allowance almost up to the stitching, but take care not to snip into the stitches themselves.

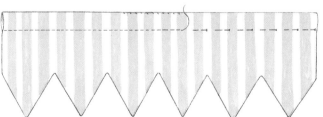

9 Turning through to right side Turn the pelmet out to the right side, using a knitting needle or darning needle to push out the points; press. Turn in the seam allowances on the top opening and slipstitch closed.

10 Making the casing Pin a straight line from the base of one side opening to the opposite side opening; stitch along line. Remove the finial from the end of one pole. Slide the pole through the casing and replace the finial.

Making individual pennants

Cutting individual pennant shapes for a window pelmet gives a range of design options. You can cut each shape in a different colour, or use just two colours and alternate them. A third option is to overlap two rows of pennants so that the ones in the back row show between the pennants in the front row.

In these instructions, each pennant is stitched, turned through to the right side and slipstitched closed. They are overlapped slightly, stitched on to a strip of Velcro, and then fixed to a standard pelmet board or valance rail.

You will need

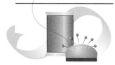

- ◆ **Fabric for pennants, front and back**
- ◆ **Matching threads**
- ◆ **Self-adhesive Velcro**
- ◆ **Bells (optional)**

1 Measuring up Measure up as for the pelmet in step **1** on page 86, bearing in mind that the shape starts at the very top of the pelmet. Divide the finished width into the required number of sections.

2 Cutting the pennants Cut a piece of paper the finished width of one pennant plus 1cm (³⁄₈in) for the overlap, by the finished depth (**B**). Fold it in half vertically; draw a line from the top corner to the bottom of the fold, and cut along the line through both layers. Open out. With the front and back fabrics right sides together, use the pattern to cut out the required number of pennants, allowing 1.5cm (⁵⁄₈in) all round.

B

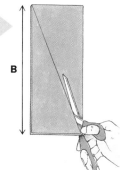

3 Stitching the pennants Stitch the two layers of each pennant right sides together, leaving a 5cm (2in) opening along the top edge of each. Trim and clip seam allowances and turn to right side. Slipstitch the opening closed; press.

▲ Contrasting plain colours are used to make a jolly clown pennant pelmet that echoes the curtain fabric, with bells jingling in the breeze.

▲ For a double row of pennants, stitch only the side seams of the shapes, then arrange them in position and stitch a narrow tape across the top raw edges. Trim the seams allowances, turn the tape to the back of the shapes and slipstitch it in place. If you wish, you can trim the top edge with braid.

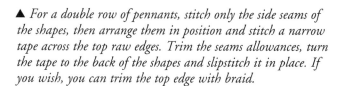

4 Assembling the pelmet Cut a piece of Velcro to finished width of the pelmet, and pin the soft side, wrong side up, to the work surface. Arrange the pennants along it, right side up, overlapping the points and with the top edges level with the top of the Velcro. Pin, tack and stitch the pennants to the Velcro, stitching 6mm (¼in) from the top.

5 Finishing off the pelmet If you wish, stitch a bell to the tip of each pennant. Then stick the hard side of the Velcro to the top edge of the pelmet board or valance rail, and hang the pelmet in place.

Versatile blinds

*There is a blind to suit every room and window – consider the
different options before decorating your window to ensure you get the
privacy, light, practicality and sheer good looks you want.*

Many people are a bit bewildered by the variety of styles available for blinds, so they stick to curtains for an easier life. However, the styles are really versions of the same thing: a blind is simply a piece of fabric hung from the top of the window, which pulls up to clear the window, rather than being pulled from the side like curtains. There are various different systems of opening and closing a blind, all creating a different effect.

In general, blinds are a neater, less obtrusive way of dressing a window, and they use less fabric, especially when compared to floor-length curtains. They have the advantage of leaving the space around the window free, making them ideal for more cluttered areas, such as kitchens and bathrooms.

In addition, the character of a blind can be totally changed by the type of fabric it's made from: a Roman blind in a sheer voile will filter the light gently and have a contemporary look; the same style in a rich damask with a lining will block the light effectively and flatter a warm, period-style room. Adding a trim or shaping the edges of the blind also lends interest and style to your room. From the basic roller blind to the exquisite festoon, there is a blind to suit every window in your house.

◀ *Roller blind A fresh green and white check is an ideal fabric for a series of conservatory roller blinds, harmonizing with the natural colour of the garden beyond and protecting the room against the sun. The shaping at the base of each blind gives an elegant finish.*

Choosing a style

The simplest type of blind, the roller blind, consists of a flat piece of fabric, stiffened and wrapped around a wooden roller which is fixed in brackets at the top of the window. The roller has a spring in one end and the blind can be fixed at any height by a ratchet system. You can make roller blinds in most fabrics, and the stiffening agent means that the surface can be wiped clean with a damp cloth, making them hygienic and practical for kitchens and bathrooms.

For a luxurious period look, a festoon blind has extra fullness which is gathered into the length, giving a rich, ruched effect, even when it's down. It is generally made with fine textures like voile, and as it uses a large quantity of fabric, it can be expensive.

A series of cords, running vertically through rings sewn on the back of the fabric, forms the basis for raising and lowering a number of different blind styles. A Roman blind pulls up in horizontal folds, kept straight by narrow rods sewn at intervals into the back of the blind. This gives a very neat, orderly effect, ideal for modern interiors, but it

is also suitable for all sorts of different situations where space is a problem.

A couple of pulleys, a length of strong cord and a cleat turn a length of fabric into a roll-up blind, which rolls up around a weighted rod slotted into the bottom. You can get interesting effects with contrast lining, which shows on the back of the blind as it rolls up.

Bundle blinds are just as the name suggests – the fabric is loosely gathered up from the bottom and held in place by decorative ties hanging at the front and back of the blind, forming a casual 'bundle' of fabric. Operating the blind is a little fiddly, so they are best used in a room where they will not have to be pulled up and down all the time.

Austrian blinds have double fullness in the width, usually gathered in with heading tape, and they bunch up into a series of pretty scoops of ruched fabric. They are a delightful style for a feminine look or for a country cottage effect.

◄ *Roman blinds Here, in a vibrant stripe, Roman blinds make a striking and adaptable window treatment for a large window in a contemporary setting. Separate blinds on each window mean you can adjust the individual height of each blind to suit your needs.*

◀ *Festoon blind* The cascading ripples of this blind accentuates the height of this tall window and adds just the right tone of elegance in a classic bathroom. It gives an overall rich and sophisticated appearance.

▶ *London blind A* delicate voile, scattered with a leafy pattern, falls across the window in a graceful scoop to gently filter the light. The design and colouring are chosen to harmonize perfectly with the daintily sprigged wallpaper.

▼ *Roll-up blind An* unusual and original effect is achieved with a richly coloured turquoise linen, lined in acid green. Matching cord completes the ensemble.

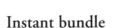

Instant bundle

Make a crisp looking blind from a linen cloth or tea towel. Hold the fabric in place with upholstery nails hammered into the window frame, starting at the outer corners. For each tie, double a length of sturdy ribbon over the top of the cloth, so it hangs down the front and back; secure with a couple of nails through all the layers. Cut the ends of each ribbon at an angle to prevent fraying. Here the towel has been rolled up before being tied in place.

HERE'S HOW

Clever and creative combinations

Mixing blinds with other types of window treatment gives more versatility and choice. Providing necessary privacy and light exclusion with a blind in a thick fabric means you can have curtains purely for decoration, if you wish. Team floaty voile full-length curtains with a thick, textured blind, or splash out on a luxurious fabric, using it for dress curtains only; drape an interesting shawl or scarf on swag holders and soften the lines of the blind; these options are often more economical than conventional curtains.

Alternatively, try making translucent blinds in voile or muslin – there are many ranges with woven or printed designs to choose from. You can make most types of blinds in fine fabrics; they make a stylish alternative to net curtains, and they combine well with with heavier curtains for warmth and privacy.

▶ *Bold stripes The broad stripes of the fabric on this Roman blind are complemented by an exotically shaped pelmet and plain curtains, in this carefully designed bedroom. The folds of the blind fall exactly along the lines of the stripes, to enhance the effect.*

◀ *Made to match Some fabric ranges make combining different patterns easy. Here, the Roman blind echoes the background colours and stripes of the curtains.*

▲ *Dainty edge The simplicity of this cream linen blind, with a delicate embroidered detail at its base, is set off by the sweeping lines of the check fabric draped over the pole.*

Roller blind

The most economical and easiest blinds to make are roller blinds. You can use them for privacy and to shade strong light, especially on windows where there isn't much space.

Neat and practical, the curvy shape at the bottom of this roller blind echoes the shaped top of the dresser prettily, and contrasts well with the brisk, checked fabric.

Making a roller blind

In many homes there are windows where curtains just do not work – over the kitchen sink, for example, or in a small bathroom, where space is cramped. The ideal solution is a roller blind – a flat panel of fabric, which rolls up out of the way when it's not needed. It is simple to make and involves very little sewing.

The blind is made of stiffened fabric which winds round a roller at the top. A wooden or plastic slat fits into a casing at the bottom, holding the lower edge straight. The roller has a spring-loaded mechanism, so you can raise and lower the blind by pulling a cord.

You can buy roller blind kits in most do-it-yourself and department stores. Specially stiffened fabric is sold in widths of up to 175cm (69in), so you can cover most windows without having to join widths. If you prefer, you can stiffen your own furnishing fabric, and coordinate the blind with curtains and soft furnishings. Stiffening solution, which also prevents fraying, is sold alongside roller blind kits. For the best results, choose a closely woven, colourfast fabric.

Fitting details

A roller blind is usually hung inside the window recess, where it fits neatly against the glass. If you want to hang yours outside the recess, make the blind 10cm (4in) longer and wider than the recess to prevent light from seeping in at the sides. When buying fabric, allow the total blind drop plus 30cm (12in).

Buy a roller blind kit to the exact width required, or the next size up. The kits include a roller, which can be cut to size, a slat for the base of the blind, two brackets, a spring-loaded winding mechanism, cord and a toggle.

If you are fixing the fittings for the roller blind into wood, you also need a bradawl and screwdriver; alternatively, to fix them into masonry you need a drill, wallplugs and a screwdriver.

You will need

- ◆ **Roller blind kit**
- ◆ **Stiffened fabric or fabric and stiffening solution**
- ◆ **Matching thread**
- ◆ **Tailor's chalk**
- ◆ **Carpenter's level**
- ◆ **Small saw and hammer**
- ◆ **Rotary cutter and cutting mat or craft knife**
- ◆ **Steel rule and set square**
- ◆ **Sticky tape**
- ◆ **Tacks or staple gun**

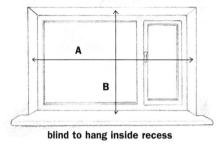

blind to hang inside recess   **blind to hang outside recess**

1 Measuring up *For a blind to hang inside recess:* measure the width of window recess (**A**) and the height from the recess to the sill (**B**). *For a blind to hang outside recess:* add 10cm (4in) to measurement **A** for **C**. Add 5cm (2in) to **B** for **D**. Buy a kit to fit the required measurements.

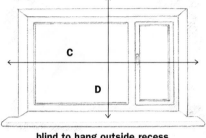

2 Fixing the brackets Follow the kit instructions to fix the brackets and use a carpenter's level to check that they are level. *For inside the recess,* fix the brackets close to the sides and at least 3cm (1¼in) below the ceiling of the recess to allow for the rolled fabric. *For outside the recess,* fit the brackets 5cm (2in) above the window, and 5cm (2in) to either side.

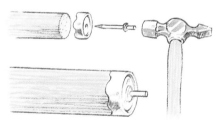

3 Trimming the roller Using the steel rule, measure between the brackets and deduct 3mm (⅛in) to allow for the end cap. Saw off the bare end of the roller to this length. Fit the cap over the sawn end, push the pin into the hole and gently hammer it home.

4 Preparing the fabric In case of any shrinkage, stiffen the fabric before cutting it. Use the fabric stiffener, following the manufacturer's instructions. Leave to dry thoroughly.

5 Calculating the size of the fabric For the width, measure the length of the roller, excluding the pin ends, and deduct 1cm (⅜in). For the length, measure from the centre of the brackets to the window sill, or to 5cm (2in) below if outside the recess; add 30cm (12in) to this measurement.

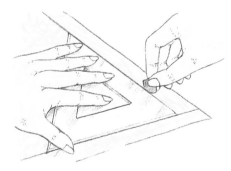

6 Cutting the fabric Lay the fabric on a flat surface, centring any large motifs or obvious pattern. Mark on the required measurements with the tailor's chalk: use a set square to get exact right angles at the corners and keep the lines on the straight grain. Using the rotary cutter or craft knife, and the steel rule as a guide, cut the fabric to the correct size.

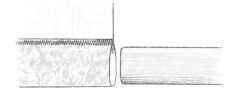

7 **Fitting the slat** Saw the slat 1cm (⅜in) shorter than the width of the blind. On the bottom edge of the blind, turn under 5cm (2in). Check that the slat fits easily inside this casing and adjust if necessary. Machine zigzag close to the edge of the casing; slide the slat in, and zigzag or oversew the ends closed.

8 **Attaching the cord** Push one end of the cord through the hole in the cord holder, and knot to secure. Thread the other end through the toggle and tie a knot. Position the holder centrally on the casing, and screw into the slat through the fabric.

9 **Aligning the roller and fabric** Lay the roller on the right side of the fabric, parallel to the upper edge. Wind the edge of the fabric on to the roller, aligning it with one of the horizontal marks. If there are no horizontal marks on the roller, draw a straight line along the roller at right angles to the edge and align the fabric with this. Fix the fabric in place temporarily with sticky tape.

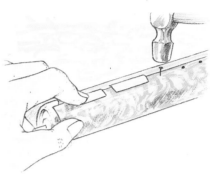

10 **Fixing the fabric** Some kits supply special tape which you use for fixing the fabric. Otherwise, hammer small tacks 2cm (⅜in) apart into the fabric edge, or use a staple gun. Peel off the sticky tape.

11 **Hanging the blind** Roll the fabric tightly round the roller and fit the roller into the brackets. Pull the blind down to its fullest extent. Tug the cord gently to see if the blind rolls up smoothly; if not, there is not enough tension. Unroll and roll again more tightly until it works properly. Adjust the cord length if necessary.

REVERSE ROLLING **Tip**
If you are using printed fabric, the wrong side will show on the roller as it rolls up, as the fabric normally drops down the back of the roller. To prevent this, reverse the bracket positions and lay the roller on the *wrong* side at step 9, so that the fabric drop hides the roller.

◀ *A plain and functional roller blind leaves you free to create purely dramatic effects with curtains – here the curtain has been swooped back to show a richly contrasting lining.*

Shaped-edge blinds

To add interest to the lower edge of a blind, you can shape it into scallops, wavy lines or zigzag points. Use a design printed on pelmet stiffening (Pelmform) as a template, or design your own.

The casing for the slat is positioned above the shaping, with the fabric turned under to form a deep hem to give body to the panel. You need to cut the blind 25cm (10in) longer to allow for this.

The cut edge won't fray, but it's best to neaten it with braid, bias binding or another flexible trim, such as gimp, which you can ease round corners and curves.

You will need

Everything listed on page 94, plus the following:

◆ **Trimming**

◆ **Double-sided fusible interfacing (Bondaweb)**

◆ **Pelmform with printed shaping lines (optional)**

◆ **Paper clips or masking tape**

◆ **Scissors and pencil**

◆ **Fabric adhesive**

1 Cutting out Prepare and cut out the blind as in steps **1-6** on page 94, but adding an extra 25cm (10in) to the length. On wrong side, measure and mark a line 5cm (2in) from the lower edge for the casing.

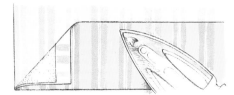

2 Turning up the hem Cut interfacing to the width of the blind by 20cm (8in) deep. Position it above the line. Following manufacturers' instructions, fuse the interfacing to the fabric. Peel off the paper backing, and fold up the hem along the top edge of the interfacing. Fuse the layers together.

▶ *This roller blind has a wavy edge which softens the effect of the bold geometric striped fabric. A yellow gimp braid conceals the edge of the blind.*

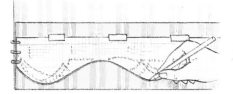

3 Cutting shaped edge Cut out your template or chosen shape printed on the Pelmform. Position along hem, on wrong side, centring design so that it finishes at same point on each edge. Secure with paper clips or masking tape. Draw round shape or template. Then cut along the shaping line.

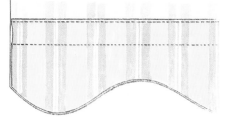

4 Stitching the casing Machine stitch close to the raw edge and again 5cm (2in) below to form the casing. Saw the slat 1cm (⅜in) shorter than the blind width. Insert it in the casing and stitch the ends closed.

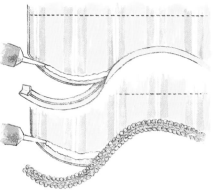

5 Adding the trimming Turning under 1cm (⅜in) at both ends, glue your chosen trim along the cut edge as follows: *For bias binding*, press in half and glue on both sides of cut edge, enclosing it. For g*imp braid*, glue along the edge on the front of the blind, overhanging the cut edge slightly to conceal it.

6 Completing the blind Follow steps **8-11** on the previous page to finish making the blind and fixing it at the window.

London blind

This simple and elegant style of blind will suit any window and grace any room. It makes the perfect alternative to curtains.

For a neat and functional window treatment, it's hard to beat the practicality of a blind, which conveniently pulls up out of the way during the day. The London blind is a beautifully streamlined version, which pleats up into a single, graceful sweep when raised, and looks smart enough for any room in the house, including a formal dining or sitting room.

The London blind has only a small amount of fullness caught into two neat box pleats at the top, giving it a soft finish, but making it far more economical on fabric than curtains or gathered blinds, such as Austrians and festoons.

To make the blind, choose a crisp, firm fabric, which holds its shape well when pleated. Checked or striped cottons suit the simplicity of the style particularly well; or you can opt for a rich damask or a lively floral print – intricate patterns will be shown off to advantage as the blind lies almost flat.

▲ *The points where the blind is ruched up call out for a decorative trim – like the silky gold tassels used here, which fill the space created by the drawn-up fabric and echo its rich design.*

You can make the blind lined or unlined, and hang it inside or outside the window recess. Apart from cord, a cleat and curtain rings, you need no special equipment – though you may want to trim the blind with tassels or fringing.

Making a London blind

The blind is simply a hemmed square of fabric with two box pleats in the top. Here the pleats lie 10cm (4in) in from the sides of the blind; you can place them slightly further in on a wider window, if desired. A fabric-covered rod is stitched to the back to stop the weight of the blind pulling it in at the sides. The blind is made 30cm (12in) longer than the window to give it a full look, even when lowered.

The blind is held at the desired height by winding the pull-cords around a cleat hook, fixed beside the window – either to the frame or to the wall.

You will need

- ◆ Furnishing fabric
- ◆ Small plastic or brass rings: 2 for every 20cm (8in) of the total drop of the blind
- ◆ Blind cord: a piece 4 times B plus 2 times A
- ◆ Length of 13mm (½in) diameter dowel rod, 20cm (8in) shorter than A
- ◆ Dressmaker's pencil, thread

For fixing:
- ◆ Wooden batten 50mm (2in) x 25mm (1in) x A
- ◆ Screws and rawlplugs for fixing the batten
- ◆ 3 screw eyes
- ◆ Cleat hook with screws, cord acorn
- ◆ Velcro equal to A in length
- ◆ 2 brackets 5 x 5cm (2 x 2in) if fixing the batten outside the window frame

1 **Calculating the size** For the blind width, add 20cm (8in) for pleats and 10cm (4in) for side hems to **A**. For the drop, add 10cm (4in) to **B**.

2 **Cutting out the fabric** Cut a piece of fabric to the required size, centring any pattern. If you need more than one width of fabric, join two half-widths on either side of a whole width, and press the seams open.

Measuring up

The blind is attached to a batten fixed either to the top of the window recess, or outside the frame if window is not recessed. Two cords run through rings up the back of the blind to screw eyes in the batten, then down to the cleat. **Inside the recess** Measure across the top of the recess and subtract 1cm (⅜in) to find the finished blind width (**A**); this is also the batten length. For the finished drop (**B**), measure from the soffit to the sill and add 30cm (12in). **Outside the recess** Make the blind the width of the window frame; for the finished length, measure from top of frame to sill, and add 30cm (12in).

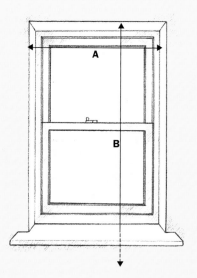

Fixing the batten

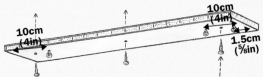

Measure 10cm (4in) in from each end of the batten and insert a screw eye centrally at these points. Insert the remaining screw eye 1.5cm (⅝in) in from the right hand end of the batten. Staple the hard side of the Velcro along the batten's front edge.

Inside the recess If fixing the batten inside the window recess, screw it up to the soffit of the recess.

Outside the frame If fixing the batten outside the frame, fix the brackets so that the batten is level with the top of the window frame.

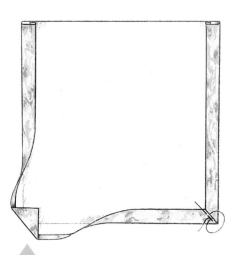

3 **Hemming the sides and base** Press under 1cm (⅜in) then 4cm (1⅝in) on the sides and base of the blind. Fold the corners of the hem in at an angle at each end until they align with the side hems. Pin and stitch the hems, close to the folds. To finish, slipstitch neatly down the folded corners.

4 **Forming the pleats** On the right side, measure the total drop **B** at intervals up from bottom of blind, and mark a line with a dressmaker's pencil. Measure 10cm (4in) in from one side along the top edge and mark with a pin; measure same amount again, and bring pins together, keeping top edges level. Repeat at other side of blind.

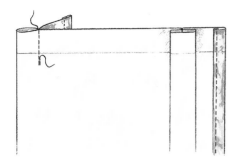

5 Stitching the pleats Pin the pleats in a vertical line from the top edge of the blind to 5cm (2in) below the marked drop line. Stitch to secure, reverse stitching at each end. Open each pleat out so that the centre fold lines up with the seamline, and press flat to form an inverted box pleat.

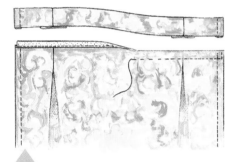

6 Adding the Velcro Lay the remaining half of the strip of Velcro right side up on right side of the blind, with its lower edge along the marked line; pin and stitch along this edge. Trim away any remaining fabric so that the raw edges are covered by the Velcro strip. Press the Velcro to the blind's wrong side. Pin and stitch along other three edges of the Velcro through all layers.

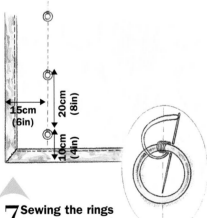

7 Sewing the rings On the wrong side, mark a line 15cm (6in) in from one side edge of the blind. Stitch the first ring on this line, 10cm (4in) up from the base edge, using double matching thread. Continue up the blind, stitching a ring at 20cm (8in) intervals; the last ring should be at least 10cm (4in) from the bottom of the pleat. Repeat up the other side of the blind.

15cm (6in)
20cm (8in)
10cm (4in)

8 Making a casing Cut a fabric strip 7cm (2¾in) wide by the batten length plus 5cm (2in). Fold in half lengthways, right sides together. Stitch the long edges and across one end taking a 1cm (⅜in) seam. Turn right side out.

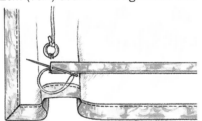

9 Attaching the batten Insert the batten into the casing and slipstitch the open end closed. Position casing to the wrong side of the blind, just below the bottom rings, and stitch each end to the blind.

10 Stringing the blind Tie one end of the cord to the bottom ring that will lie furthest from the cleat when the blind is hung in place. Thread it through all the rings directly above, and leave the end long enough to stretch across the top of the blind and down to the cleat, plus 30cm (12in). Repeat with the remaining cord on the other side of the blind.

▲ *The simple lines of a London blind are the perfect foil for attention-seeking fabrics – like this merry floral print. The pleats are cleverly arranged to gather in two complete stripes, so that the fabric design remains undisturbed.*

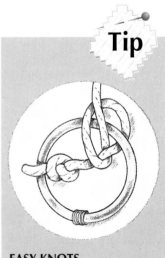

Tip

EASY KNOTS
To tie the cord securely to the bottom rings, make a single knot in the end of the cord, then a single knot on the ring. Pull tight against the first knot.

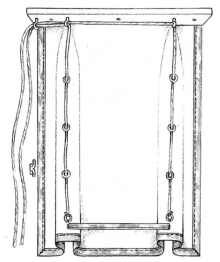

11 Hanging the blind Press the Velcro at the top of the blind to the Velcro on the batten. Thread the cord furthest from cleat, through the screw eye above it and across the top through the other two screw eyes; take remaining cord through the second and third screw eyes. Pull on the cords until the blind is fully up, ensuring the two sides are hanging evenly; knot the cords level with the cleat to fix blind in the up position.

12 Attaching the pull Allow the blind to drop so the bottom edge forms a gentle curve which just clears the sill at the centre. Thread the pull on to the cords and knot below the pull, level with the cleat. Trim off the cord below the knot.

13 Dressing in the folds For a neat finish, run your fingers along the folds, pulling them out fully to fall forward over one another. Allow the folds to 'set' for a couple of days before lowering the blind.

▶ *Elegant and understated, London blinds in a straightforward two-colour check to match the walls introduce a subtle softening influence into this sitting room, without disturbing its unfussy appeal.*

Lined London blind

Lining makes the blind more substantial and gives a more professional finish; it also helps to cut out light and insulate the room more efficiently. Allow the same amount of lining as main fabric.

1 Cutting out Measure and cut out the fabric as in steps **1-2** of *Making a London blind*. Cut the lining 10cm (4in) narrower and 5cm (2in) shorter than the fabric.

2 Adding the lining With wrong sides together, lay the lining centrally on the fabric with the bottom 5cm (2in) above the bottom of the fabric, and 5cm (2in) of fabric showing at each side. Press the side and bottom hem allowances in over the lining. Pin and stitch in place, enclosing the edges of the lining. To finish the blind, follow steps **4-13** of *Making a London blind*, treating both the fabric layers as one.

Bundle blinds

Soft and casual, bundle blinds have a look that's perfect for today's simple interiors, and they're very easy to make. Add contrasting linings and interesting ties, and they can be decorative too.

Bundle blinds are very easy to make from ... which ... from the top ... of ties are s ... rectangle, ha ... behind. To r ... gather it up in ... ties beneath ...

... lcro to a narrow ...op. These blinds ...ional use, rather ...re you need to ...y day, as it can ... operation. ...rly look, stitch ...bottom, so you ...d the rod. This

can look very effective if you use a contrasting or toning lining, which will be displayed as you roll the blind forward.

▼ *Setting the blinds at half mast gives you the opportunity to show off a semi-sheer fabric or a pretty pattern, whether the blind is hanging straight or is attractively bunched.*

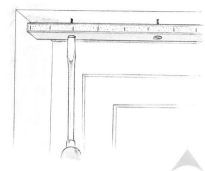

Making a bundle blind

To make and fix a wooden batten with Velcro on the front see page 98, but omit the screw eyes. When you screw it in place, leave a gap between the batten and the soffit so you can thread the ties between them.

When calculating fabric quantities, all you need for the blind is a piece of fabric 5cm (2in) bigger all round than the window recess. The fabric for the ties needs to be 36cm (14¼in) wide and the same length as the blind fabric.

You will need

- Furnishing fabric for the blind
- Furnishing fabric for the ties
- Matching thread
- 50 x 25mm (2 x 1in) batten
- Screws for fixing the batten
- Velcro

▼ *Try interesting colour combinations, such as bright blue with lime green, or pale yellow with dusky pink. Create stunning effects with the ties and lining using contrasting colours and fabrics.*

1 Measuring up Start by measuring the width (**A**) and the height (**B**) of the window recess.

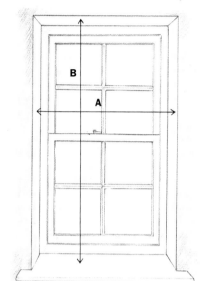

2 Fixing the batten Cut and fix the batten as on page 98, driving the screws only half-way in.

3 Cutting out *For the blinds:* cut a rectangle of fabric measuring **A** plus 7cm (2¾in) by **B** plus 6cm (2¼in). *For the ties:* cut four 9cm (3½in) wide strips the same length as the fabric.

4 Hemming the edges On the sides and base, press under 1cm (⅜in) then 2.5cm (1in); pin. Stitch close to inner fold, mitring the corners neatly.

5 Adding the Velcro Measure and mark the finished length up from the bottom edge; press to crease. Referring to page 99, step **6**, stitch the Velcro in place.

6 Making ties Right sides together, join short ends of two tie strips. Stitch long edges right sides together, leaving an opening in middle. Centre seam and press open. Stitch short ends, turn out and press. Slipstitch opening closed.

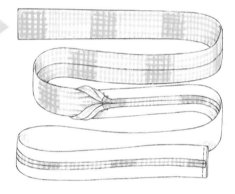

7 Finishing off Slip each tie over the top of the batten, 15cm (6in) from sides; make sure they hang equally at front and behind. Tighten the screws to secure the batten. Press the blind in place on the Velcro. Bundle up the blind from the base, knotting the ties to hold fabric in position.

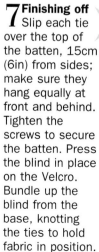

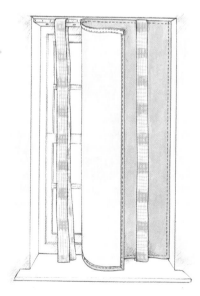

Roman blind

*Crisply pleated into neat horizontal folds, a Roman
blind has the pared down, functional look that's perfect for
a modern home, and is very economical on fabric too.*

This neat and elegant blind looks very simple from the front, falling in a series of level folds to the sill. But behind the streamlined pleats, a clever system of rods, slipped into casings at the back of the blind, holds the folds straight. The blind is easily raised and lowered by pulling or releasing cords; these cords run through rings stitched to the casings.

Roman blinds hang completely flat when lowered, so they use very little fabric. To ensure a professional finish and a neat fit, it is very important to measure up and stitch as accurately as possible, particularly at the base edge.

Kits and accessories

Roman blind kits include everything you need except the fabric and rods, and are available in two sizes. You can also buy all the components separately.

Blind cord and small curtain rings in brass or plastic are available from curtain accessory departments. Rings are stitched to the casings to carry the cords. To work out how many rings you need, multiply the number of casings by the number of cords required. Each cord should be the width of the blind plus twice the length.

As a short cut, you can buy special Roman blind tape. This is a ready-made casing with loops at intervals which cuts out the need for stitching on rings.

Rods and base lath You need one rod for every casing. Special plastic rods, that you can cut or extend to size, are available as an extra to the blind kits, or you can buy 6mm (¼in) diameter wooden dowel from hardware and do-it-yourself shops. The bottom edge of the blind is held straight by a base lath. You can buy a plastic lath or use a 25 x 3mm (1 x ⅛in) wooden lath. Cut the rods and base lath 2cm (¾in) shorter than the finished width of the blind.

◀ *This blind has no rings on the bottom section, so it hangs down, even when the other sections are folded up. To allow the maximum amount of light into a room, stitch extra rings to the hem of a blind.*

Measuring up

The top of the blind is fixed to a batten with Velcro in the same way as a London blind. The batten can be fixed to the top of the window recess, or outside the frame if the window is not recessed.

Inside the recess Measure across the top of the recess and subtract 1cm (⅜in) for the finished blind width (**A**). For the finished length (**B**), measure from the top of the recess to the sill and subtract 6mm (¼in).

Outside the frame Make the blind the width of the window frame (**A**); for the finished length (**B**), measure from the top of the batten to the sill, and subtract 6mm (¼in).

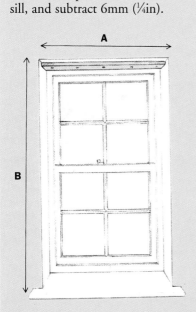

Batten fitted in window recess

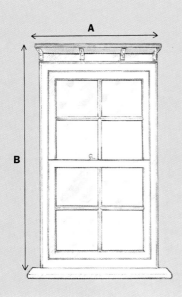

Batten fitted outside window frame

Making an unlined Roman blind

This simple method uses the main fabric to make the rod casings. Choose a plain fabric or a pattern, such as a stripe, which has no obvious vertical repeat to be interrupted by the casings. You can also use this method to make sheer Roman blinds in voile or fine cotton.

Join panels of fabric to make up the required width; add extra panels each side of a central width to avoid a centre seam. For blinds wider than 80cm (31½in), space extra cords and rings at equal intervals between the outer ones.

You will need

◆ **Furnishing fabric**

◆ **Small rings**

◆ **Blind cord**

◆ **Rods**

◆ **Base lath**

◆ **Dressmaker's pencil, pins**

For fixing:

◆ **50 x 25mm (2 x 1in) wooden batten length of A**

◆ **Screws and rawlplugs for fixing the batten**

◆ **Screw eyes**

◆ **Cleat hook with screws**

◆ **Cord pull**

◆ **Velcro equal to A in length**

◆ **If fixing the blind outside the window frame – two brackets 5 x 5cm (2 x 2in)**

1 Cutting the fabric Straighten the cut end of the fabric. *For the width*, add 10cm (4in) to **A**. *For the length*, add 5cm (2in) for each casing plus 12cm (4¾in) for seam allowances to **B**. Cut one piece of your main fabric to these measurements. If necessary, join the side panels with flat fell seams to make up the required width.

2 Hemming the sides Press under 1cm (⅜in), then 4cm (1⅝in) on both side edges of the blind. Pin and stitch the hems close to the fold.

The number of rod casings depends on the length of the blind – as a rough guide, insert one casing every 25-30cm (10-12in). When you are buying the fabric, allow an extra 5cm (2in) for each casing, plus 10cm (4in) for turnings for each drop.

Fixing the batten

Make up and fix a batten with screw eyes and Velcro as on page 98. Fix the cleat at a comfortable height to one side of the window frame.

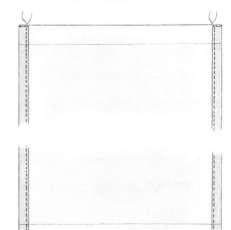

3 Marking the top and base On the wrong side, mark a line 1cm (⅜in), then a second line 5cm (2in) up from the lower edge – the second marks the base line. Lightly draw a line 10cm (4in) down from top edge – this allows 4cm (1½in) extra depth in the top fold.

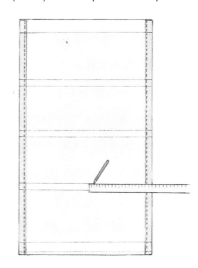

4 Marking the casings Divide the space between the base line and the top line into equal sections of about 30-35cm (12-13¾in) and mark them with horizontal lines. For the casings, draw parallel lines 5cm (2in) above each of these lines.

The pleats on a Roman blind can be as wide as you wish; remember, though, that the narrower the pleats are the more they will bunch up together when the blind is raised.

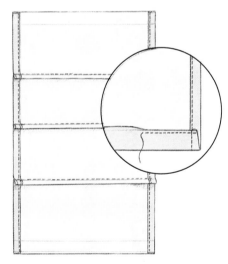

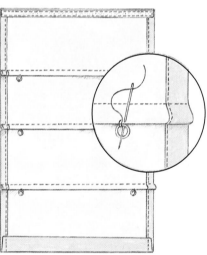

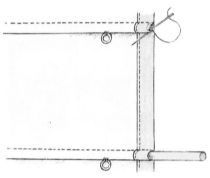

7 Inserting the rods Slide a rod into each casing, and base lath into base hem. Slipstitch ends closed. String the blind as on page 99, step **10**.

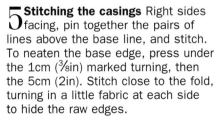

5 Stitching the casings Right sides facing, pin together the pairs of lines above the base line, and stitch. To neaten the base edge, press under the 1cm (⅜in) marked turning, then the 5cm (2in). Stitch close to the fold, turning in a little fabric at each side to hide the raw edges.

6 Adding Velcro and rings Measure finished length from base of blind; mark new top line. Apply soft side of Velcro, as on page 99, step **6**. Using double thread, sew a ring to the folded edge of each casing, 10cm (4in) in from each side, and at regular intervals in between on wider blinds.

8 Hanging the blind Hang the blind as on page 100, steps **11-12**, threading the cords through the screw eyes, then through the pull. Pull the blind up as far as it will go and check that the folds are level; drop the blind and knot the cords below the pull, level with the cleat.

Lined Roman blind

With all the casings made in the lining, a lined Roman blind shows off patterns splendidly – all you see from the front are single rows of stitching, securing the casings to the main fabric. On a plain fabric you could turn this into a feature by using a brightly contrasting thread – red stitching on cream calico, for instance. Make sure that your stitching is straight, though, as wobbly lines will spoil the hang and appearance.

Calculate the amount of lining as for the main fabric on the previous page. For the main fabric, add an extra 10cm (4in) to the finished length to allow for turnings. All the other materials are the same as for an unlined Roman blind.

▶ *Use a lining to add body to a lightweight fabric, so that the blind hangs down in crisp pleats.*

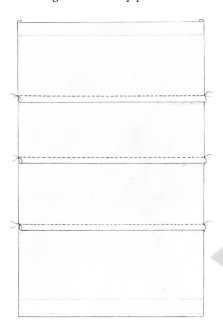

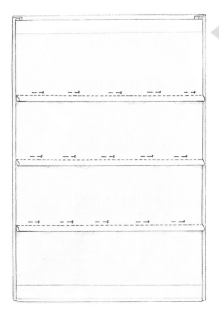

1 **Cutting out** Referring to *Measuring up* on the previous page, cut a piece of fabric **A** plus 10cm (4in) by **B** plus 12cm (4¾in). Cut the lining to exactly the width of **A** by the fabric length plus 5cm (2in) for each casing.

2 **Preparing the lining** On both side edges of the lining, press under 1cm (⅜in). *Working on the right side*, follow steps **3-5** on the previous pages to mark the base, top and casings, and stitch casings *wrong sides together*.

3 **Attaching the lining** On the side edges of the fabric, press under 5cm (2in). Wrong sides together, centre the lining on the fabric. Pin and tack across the blind just above each casing. Matching bobbin thread to fabric and top thread to lining, stitch along the tacked lines.

4 **Slipstitching the sides** Slipstitch side edges of lining to the fabric, leaving casings open. Press under the base as in step **5**, previous page, then open out and trim away the lining at base line before stitching in place.

5 **Completing the blind** Follow steps **6-8** on the previous page to complete the blind, treating the fabric and lining as one at the top edge.

Tip

CORD CONNECTORS
A wide blind may have too many cords to fit inside the pull. Thread all the cords through the top hole of a plastic cord connector, knot together and trim off all but one. Thread through the base and screw together.

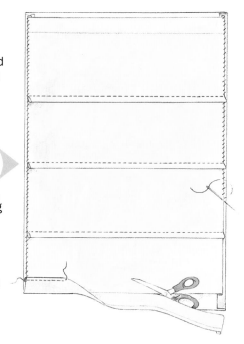

Tailored tiebacks

Tiebacks neatly finish off your curtains to perfection.
They sweep the curtains into an elegant curve, drawing them
away from the window to let more light in.

Professional look-ing tiebacks are easy to achieve using only a small amount of fabric – you need about 1m (1⅛yd) for each pair.

You can use a remnant of fabric left over from making the curtains, or choose a coordinating fab-ric to make the tiebacks stand out. Plain fabric tiebacks are effective against a patterned print – pick a colour in the curtain design and link it with upholstery or accessories in the room. Or you can choose a complemen-tary pattern – dashing black and white checks on curtains made of traditional ticking, or leafy sprigs to coordinate with a large floral.

For a lively new look with plain curtains, you can add a dash of pat-tern – try floral chintz on plain cotton. You can even use lace, if you back it with a toning fabric.

◀ *Using a colourful patterned fabric to make a tieback for a plain curtain livens up the whole window dressing.*

Making a tieback

The trace-off pattern below is a template for half a tieback. When cutting out the fabric, lining and interlining, place the straight edge along the fold. Use the whole newspaper pattern for cutting out the stiff buckram that does not fold easily. The finished tieback measures 65cm (25½in) long by 10cm (4in) wide.

The tiebacks are stiffened with buckram – a thick canvas impregnated with starch – or you can use heavy iron-on interfacing. For a really professional finish, a layer of interlining, such as bump, domette or fleece, between the fabric and the buckram gives a softer touch and gently rounds the edges of the tieback. For the back, use the same fabric or economise with lining fabric.

If the fabric you are using has an obvious design, position the tieback pattern carefully on the fabric, so that a large flower motif occurs in the middle of the tieback for instance. You can place stripes either vertically, to blend with the fabric, or horizontally to contrast.

place along fold

1 Measuring up
Loop a tape measure around the curtain to hold it back neatly but not too tightly. Read off the measurement to get the length of the tieback.

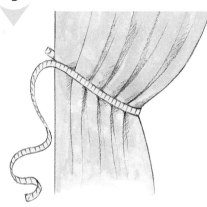

2 Making a pattern Trace all pattern lines on to tracing paper. Fold a sheet of newspaper in half and place the straight edge of the pattern along the fold and transfer the cutting lines to the newspaper. Cut round the outer broken line.
Note: When cutting out the fabric for a tieback longer than 65cm (25½in), set the pattern paper away from the fold by half the extra length.

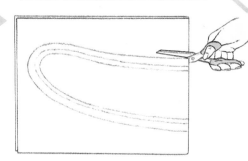

3 Cutting out
Open out the paper pattern and cut two pieces in fabric. Trim the pattern to the second broken line and cut two pieces in interlining and two in fabric or lining. Trim the pattern to the solid line and cut two pieces in buckram.

cutting line for buckram
cutting line for interlining and lining
cutting line for fabric

4 Interlining the buckram For each tieback, lay the buckram, fusible side up, centrally on an interlining piece. Fold the edges of the interlining round the sides of the buckram, snipping into them so they lie flat round the inner curves. At the ends, cut small notches in the interlining to reduce bulk. Use the tip of a warm iron to fuse the interlining in place, without letting the iron touch the buckram.

5 Adding the fabric Lay the front fabric piece, wrong side up, on the ironing board and position the buckram with its interlined surface down centrally on top. Fold the fabric over the interlining, snipping the edges so that they fit smoothly round the curves. Use the tip of a warm iron as before, to secure it to the buckram.

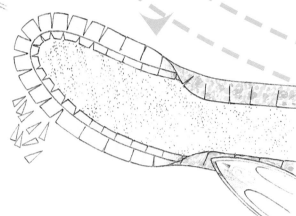

▶ *A checked fabric that coordinates with the curtain makes the ideal tieback for a simple window treatment. The chunky fringing is also in keeping with the country style and accentuates the outline of the tieback most effectively.*

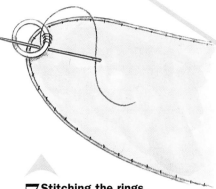

6 Adding the back piece

Clip the seam allowance of the back piece, then press it to the wrong side. Pin the back piece, wrong sides together, on the back of the tieback, covering all the raw edges neatly. Using matching thread, slipstitch the back in place.

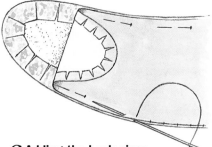

7 Stitching the rings

Using double thread, sew one curtain ring to the wrong side of each end of the tieback, making stitches close together over the ring and into the fabric. If required, stitch fringing in place along the lower edge of the tieback.

8 Fixing the tiebacks

Determine the height of the tieback hooks and fix them to the wall level with the back edge of each curtain. Wrap a tieback round each curtain.

PROFESSIONAL FINISH

Tip

To improve the hang of the tieback and curtain, set one ring in from the front edge of the tieback so that only a little of it shows from the front. On the end that sits behind the curtain, position the ring on the very edge. Use two hooks to hang the tiebacks, securing one hook a little bit in from the back edge of the curtain and the other level with the back edge.

Positioning tiebacks

Tiebacks suit all curtain lengths. It's important to position the tiebacks at the right point to flatter the proportions of the window and let in the right amount of light. The illustrations below show how to position tiebacks on sill-length, below-the-sill and full-length curtains.

▶ *Measured up and positioned correctly, a tieback gently lifts the curtain off the window. Here, a checked tieback stands out just as clearly on an all-over patterned fabric as similar checks did against the plain curtain on the previous page.*

Sill-length curtains Tiebacks placed about two-thirds of the way down sill-length curtains part them in gentle folds on either side to frame the window and let in plenty of light. Use the same proportions for below-the-sill curtains.

Placed high Positioned one-third of the way down from the top of the curtain, the tiebacks let in more light and give the impression the window is of greater length.

Sill-height tiebacks On floor-length curtains at a small window, with the tiebacks arranged at sill height, the fabric is swept into generous curves above the tiebacks and hangs down well below.

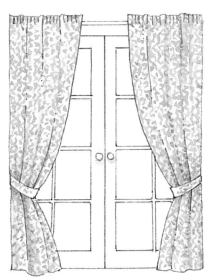

Placed low Tiebacks set two-thirds of the way down the curtain create a full effect at the top which makes a narrow window seem wider but may cut out a lot of natural light.

Piped tiebacks

Adding piping to the edge of a plain or shaped tieback gives a crisp outline and adds eye-catching detail. You can use the same technique to edge your tiebacks with smart flanged cord.

Piping defines the outline of tiebacks, helping them stand out from the curtain fabric. It adds flair and a very neat, professional finish to simple tieback styles, and accentuates the more unusual lines of shaped tiebacks – like the elegant, pointed one shown here.

When choosing your piping fabric, bring along a swatch of both your tieback and curtain fabrics (if different) to be sure of achieving a good balance. You can opt for crisp, plain piping to set off patterned fabrics; or vice versa, adding just a touch of pattern with piping in a small-scale print, fine stripes or mini-checks.

As an alternative to piping, consider trimming your tiebacks with flanged cord. This is furnishing cord stitched to a narrow strip of cotton tape, which is caught in the seam when you make up the tieback, in the same way as piping. Fabric and sewing stores stock a wide range of flanged trims, so you will have no trouble in finding one that's just right for your fabrics.

Full size pattern

You will find it easier to cut out the tieback, and position any design motifs in the main fabric, if you use a complete pattern, rather than one that needs to be placed on a fold. You also need a full size pattern for cutting out the buckram, as it is far too thick to fold in half.

▶ *A fine line of flanged cord defines the outline of this shaped tieback, which sweeps down to a centre point. A small, silky tassel, stitched to the point, makes an elegant detail.*

Making a piped tieback

You will need

For one pair of tiebacks:

◆ 50cm (⁵/₈yd) of furnishing fabric

◆ 50cm (⁵/₈yd) of lining fabric

◆ 50cm (⁵/₈yd) of contrast fabric for piping

◆ 50cm (⁵/₈yd) of fusible buckram or heavyweight fusible interfacing

◆ 50cm (⁵/₈yd) of interlining

◆ About 2m (2¹/₂yd) of piping cord

◆ Tracing paper and pencil

◆ Newspaper or brown paper

◆ Matching thread

◆ Four curtain rings

◆ Tailor's chalk

◆ Needle and pins

◆ Tieback hooks

◆ Scissors

1 Making the pattern Measure up for the tieback as on page 108, step **1**, and trace the tieback pattern provided on to tracing paper, marking along the solid (buckram) cutting line only. Transfer pattern on to a folded sheet of paper as on page 108, step **2**, and cut it out. This is the finished size of the tieback, without seam allowances.

2 Cutting out For each tieback, cut out one piece in furnishing fabric and one in lining, adding a 1.5cm (⁵/₈in) seam allowance all round. Cut out one piece in buckram and one in interlining without adding seam allowances.

4 Making the piping Make up or buy enough piping to go all round each tieback, plus 10cm (4in) for the join. When cutting the fabric strips for the piping, be sure to cut them on the true bias of the fabric, so the piping will have sufficient ease to follow the tieback curves as closely as possible.

5 Attaching the piping Lay the buckram shape centrally on the right side of the fabric piece. Draw round the outline on to the fabric with tailor's chalk, then lift off the buckram. Starting on a straight or gently curved section, apply piping so the stitching line follows the chalked line. Clip seam allowances where necessary and join the ends.

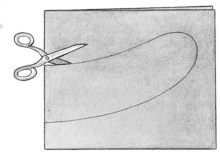

3 Fusing the buckram Lay the interlining on the fusible side of the buckram and fuse in place with a warm iron.

Fitting fabric round curves and corners

In sewing projects which involve stitching around curves, corners and points, the seam allowances won't naturally lie flats and need clipping to achieve a smooth finish.

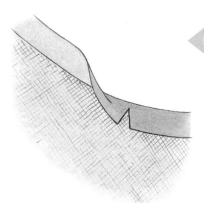

Snipping allowances Where the seam allowance has to stretch to cover a bigger space – for example, turned back on an inward curve, like the one on the top edge of a tieback – snip it with scissors, almost to the seamline, to allow the allowance to open out more.

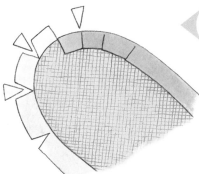

Clipping out notches Where the seam allowance has to cover a smaller space – for example, turned back on an outward curve, like those at the ends of a tieback – cut out little notches to reduce the amount of fabric.

Trimming points Trim away seam allowance at an angle, as shown, to reduce bulk.

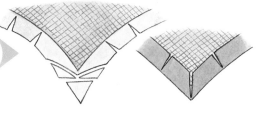

▶ *Contrast piping defines the outline of this tieback, made from the same fabric as the curtain. Use a plain fabric for the covered piping, chosen to match one of the colours in the main curtain fabric.*

6 Covering the buckram
Lay the piped fabric piece wrong side up, and fit the buckram, interlined side down, inside it, bringing the seam allowances over the edges. Clip and notch the seam allowances where necessary, so they lie flat.

7 Adding the lining On the lining piece, press 1.5cm (⅝in) to the wrong side all round, clipping and notching as necessary to get a smooth line. Wrong sides together, pin the lining to the back of the tieback, covering all the raw edges. Using matching thread, slipstitch the lining in place along the seamline.

8 Finishing off Stitch the rings in place and fix the tiebacks as on page 109, steps **7-8**.

Pointed tieback

Use the pattern template below to adapt the basic tieback pattern on pages 108–109 to make an elegant pointed tieback. Emphasize its unusual shape with a line of slim flanged cord or piping. You will need the same materials as for the piped tieback; replace the piping fabric and cord with flanged cord, if preferred.

The neat outlines of a pointed tieback make it the perfect partner for this formal yellow and white striped fabric. A matching yellow flanged cord and elaborate tassel add a professional finish.

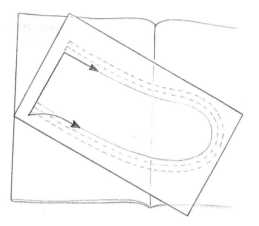

1 Tracing the pattern Trace the pointed tieback pattern given here on to tracing paper. Lay the tracing over the tieback pattern on pages 108–109, matching it up to the foldline and the solid lines. Trace off the rest of the tieback, and cut out.

2 Making the pattern Transfer the tieback pattern on to a folded sheet of paper, as on page 108, step **2**, and cut it out. This is the finished size without seam allowances.

3 Cutting out Cut out and fuse the tieback pieces as in *Making a piped tieback*, steps **2** and **3**, page 112. Follow step **5** to mark a chalk line on the right side of the main fabric piece.

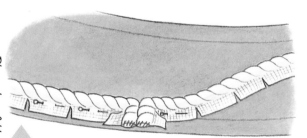

Place along fold

4 Attaching flanged cord Starting at the centre of one long edge, pin and stitch the flanged cord along the chalked line, clipping the cord tape where necessary around curves and at the point. At join, oversew ends of cord to stop them fraying, and bend them sharply down into the seam, side by side. Alternatively, apply piping.

5 Finishing off the tieback Fit the buckram and attach the lining as in steps **6-8** on the previous page.

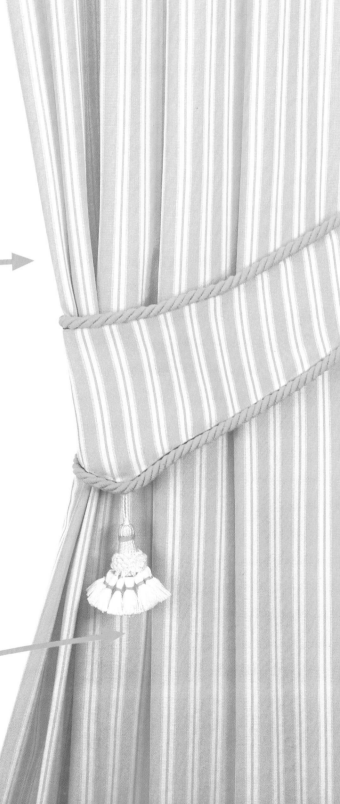

Tieback variations

*Unusual shapes and different finishing techniques,
based on the basic tailored and piped tiebacks, provide a
gallery of tieback designs for you to choose from.*

Once you are familiar with the basic construction techniques of making tiebacks, you can create a wide range of styles guaranteed to turn a plain pair of curtains into a real feature. The tiebacks on the next three pages are all variations of the basic tiebacks demonstrated on pages 108–114.

Give full rein to your flights of fancy with a prettily waved edge, for example – the perfect partner to sweet florals or dainty voiles. You could accentuate the shape with contrast piping or a flanged cord; a few silk flowers add the final flourish. For a completely different look, add a row of unusual buttons, metal studs, tiny rosettes or even shells.

For a more tailored tieback, choose an elegant, simple shape with neat, pointed ends, and play up the clean lines by binding the edges in a contrast fabric. A smart covered button in the binding fabric completes the look.

A simple shape is always successful with stripes or busy prints, but could equally well take on a sense of grandeur in gold damask, bound with cream satin and sporting a rich creamy tasselled rosette, instead of a sober button.

▶ *A thick, twisted cord in three coordinating tones of pink, cream and green, emphasizes the graceful, undulating edge of this elegant tieback. The tieback is made up in a timeless floral print that perfectly complements a classic curtain like this red velvet drape.*

Making a bound tieback

Bound edges have a lovely neat look and make a bolder statement than piping. It's a quick and easy technique, as all the layers can be cut to the same size – the binding covers the raw edges. Cutting the binding strips on the bias is very important for flexibility around the curves. You can buy ready-made bias binding from haberdashery stores, in two widths and a variety of colours, in either cotton or a shiny satin version. The tieback shown here is trimmed with 2.5cm (1in) wide binding, which finishes 1.2cm (½in) wide.

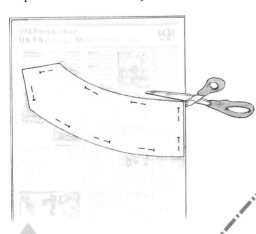

1 Cutting out Trace the tieback pattern from this page and cut it out. Fold the newspaper in half, place the straight edge of the pattern on the fold, cut round the pattern and open it out. For each tieback, use the newspaper pattern to cut one piece in fabric, buckram, lining and interlining.

2 Interlining the buckram Apply the interlining to one side of the buckram as in step **3**, page 112.

place along fold

bound tieback

wavy-edged tieback

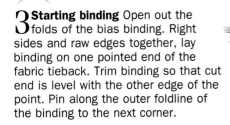

3 Starting binding Open out the folds of the bias binding. Right sides and raw edges together, lay binding on one pointed end of the fabric tieback. Trim binding so that cut end is level with the other edge of the point. Pin along the outer foldline of the binding to the next corner.

4 Pinning round the shape At the corner, make a tapered pleat in the binding, pin in place and then continue round the shape, easing the binding to fit the curve. Test the fullness as you go by turning the binding back over the pins to check that it will lie flat.

5 Continuing the binding Repeat step **4** to make pleats at the other corners, and a deeper pleat at the end point, and then continue pinning the binding along the top edge.

6 Joining ends
At the join, raise the first end of the bias binding so that you can continue pinning the other end up to the seamline. Cut off the remainder 1.2cm (½in) beyond the end point to create an overlap.

7 Stitching binding
Tack along the pinned line, then machine stitch in place, breaking the stitching at the end point to leave the pleat free.

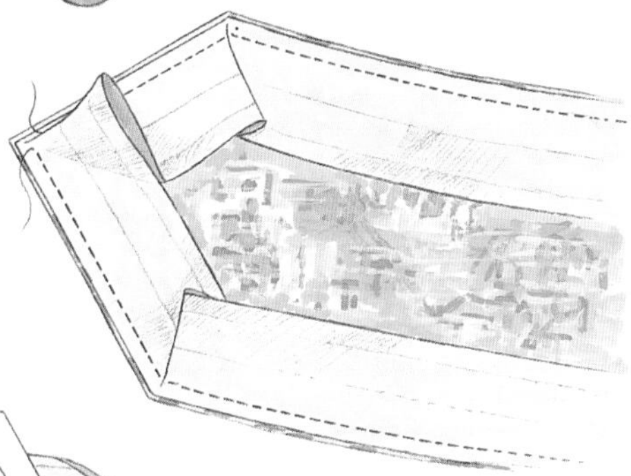

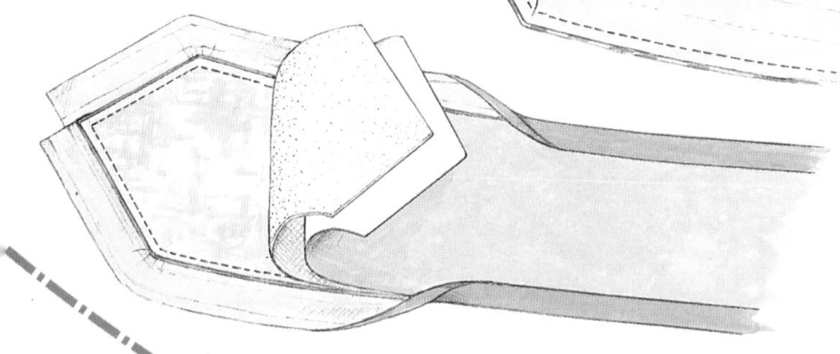

8 Assembling the tieback Lay the bound fabric piece down, with the wrong side up. Lay the buckram, interlined side down, inside it, and then place the lining on top, wrong side down. Bring the binding over the buckram and lining, enclosing all the raw edges, and then turn the raw edge of the binding in at the pressed fold.

bound tieback

wavy-edged tieback

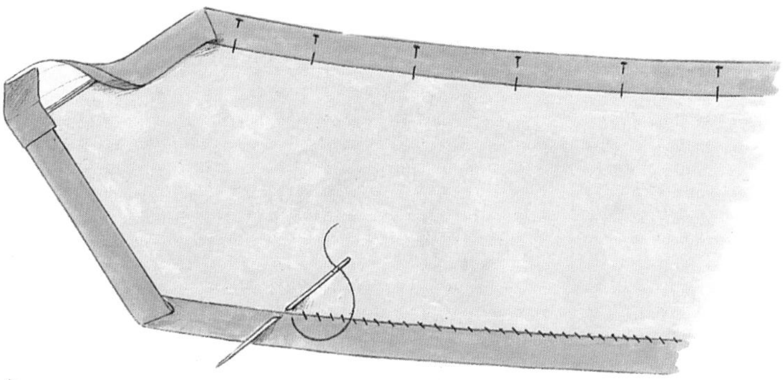

▲ *This elegant tieback is bound in a deep blue to highlight the blue in the pattern on the tieback fabric, and to create a strong contrast with the plain red curtain.*

9 Pinning the other side Pin the bias binding in place, pleating it at the corners to match the front (see steps **3-5**). At the join, turn in the 1.2cm (½in) overlap before bringing it over to enclose the first end. Matching thread to binding, slipstitch the binding in place on the back.

10 Finishing the tieback Following the manufacturer's instructions, make up a covered button in the binding fabric; sew in place on the end of the tieback which will show. Stitch the curtain rings in place and fix the tiebacks as in steps **7-8**, page 109.

Making the wavy-edged tieback

The undulating bottom edge of this tieback adds an unusual touch to your window, and is shown off to full effect by a strongly contrasting piping. Use a narrow piping cord and a closely woven fabric for the piping to make fitting round the inner curves easier.

See pages 111–113 for more instructions on making a piped tieback.

You will need

For one pair of tiebacks:

◆ 50cm (⅝yd) of furnishing fabric

◆ 50cm (⅝yd) of lining fabric (or use the same fabric)

◆ 50cm (⅝yd) of contrast fabric for piping

◆ 4m (4½yd) of piping cord

◆ 50cm (⅝yd) of fusible buckram or heavyweight fusible interfacing

◆ 50cm (⅝yd) of interlining

◆ Matching thread

◆ Four curtain rings

◆ Tailor's chalk

◆ Needle and pins

◆ Tracing paper and newspaper for pattern

1 Cutting out Using the template on the previous page, and following the lines for the wavy-edged tieback, make a pattern as in step **1**, page 112. Then follow step **2** to cut out the pieces of fabric, lining, buckram and interlining.

2 Making the piping Make up or buy enough piping to go all round each tieback, plus 10cm (4in) for the join. When cutting the strips, be sure to cut on the true bias for good flexibility round the curves.

▶ *This delightfully pretty tieback makes the most of the curtain's floral theme. The tieback is made in plain blue cotton, edged with bright yellow piping, and embellished with fabric daisies.*

3 Attaching the piping Follow the instructions in step **5**, page 112, to attach the piping. Ease the piping round the outer curves, stretch very slightly round the inner curves and clip, if necessary, as you pin. Stitch, joining the piping.

4 Adding the buckram Continue with step **6** on page 113 to cover the buckram with the tieback fabric. To get a snug fit round the curves, snip into the seam allowances and cut notches out of both the piping and the fabric, following the guidelines in *Fitting fabric round curves and corners,* page 112.

5 Completing the tiebacks Follow steps **7-8**, page 113, to add the lining and curtain rings. On the right side of the tieback, position a silk flower just above each wave, and secure in place with a few stitches.

Padded tube tiebacks

*The soft, rounded shapes created by thickly padded tubes
of fabric can really spark up a pair of plain curtains. They make
an eye-catching accessory with a contemporary feel.*

These chunky tube tiebacks have a really unusual look, and will add interest and elegance to any room. Try the double padded tube tieback shown here, or experiment with one of the many possible variations – such as a single, extra-long tube with an elaborate central knot; a tightly twisted double tube; or one with a fancy ruched finish. Instructions for all these versions are given on the following pages.

Make your padded tube tiebacks in the same fabric as the curtains for a sense of understated sophistication, or pick out one or two colours from the curtain print for an effective contrast. Their curves show off the glint and gleam of luxury fabrics, such as silks and heavy satins, and help to highlight the textures of fabrics with interesting weaves, such as jaquards and damasks.

The tiebacks are made from long tubes of fabric, padded to give plenty of body. They can be filled in a variety of ways. Some shops sell jumbo cording, made of reconstituted paper fibre, or jumbo piping, made of wadding enclosed in a stockinette tube. These are about 2.5cm (1in) in diameter, but are not always easy to get.

Alternatively, you can use up scraps of wadding or curtain interlining, rolling them up and oversewing along the edge. This method is by far the most flexible – you can make the roll as thick as you like. Wadding gives a squishier effect, but as it may flatten a little, you should roll it as tightly as you can. Interlining gives a firmer finish.

◀ *Two long, thick rolls of fabric, secured at the centre with two shorter rolls, add importance to the curtains. Their shape is made especially noticeable by the use of a single, strong dark colour, picked out from the curtain print.*

Making a tube tieback

The double tube tieback consists of two long, fabric-covered tubes, with two shorter tubes wrapped around the centre and secured at the back. The steps below give instructions for making the tubes from strips of rolled-up interlining, with a diameter of about 4cm (1½in). If you prefer to use wadding, test-roll a sample first to see what width you should cut the wadding pieces (see step **1** below).

The finished tieback measures about 90cm (35½in) long. For each tieback you will need approximately 1.2m (1¼yd) of interlining, and 0.5m (⅝yd) of fabric, depending on the width of your chosen fabric.

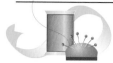

You will need

- ◆ **Furnishing fabric**
- ◆ **Interlining**
- ◆ **Matching thread**
- ◆ **Two brass curtain rings for each tieback**
- ◆ **Scissors**
- ◆ **Needle and pins**

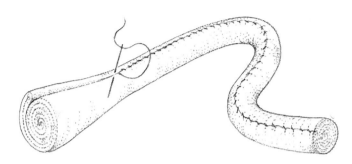

1 Making the long rolls *For each tieback:* cut two strips of interlining, 90 x 40cm (35½ x 15¾in). Fold each strip in half lengthways. Tightly roll the cut edges into the centre to form a roll about 4cm (1½in) in diameter; pin, then oversew in place along edge.

2 Making the short rolls *For each tieback:* cut two strips of interlining, 38 x 40cm (15 x 15¾in). Fold and roll both strips up tightly, as described in step **1**.

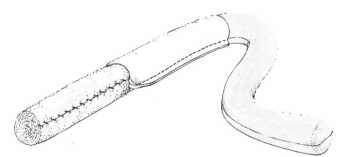

3 Making the fabric tubes Measure the length of each roll. Then, for each roll, cut a strip of fabric 6cm (2¼in) longer than the roll, by 16cm (6¼in). With right sides together, bring the long edges together to make a tube; pin and stitch the long edge and one short edge.

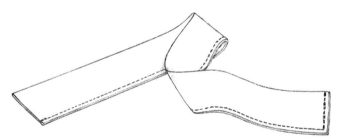

4 Covering the rolls Push the stitched end of each fabric tube inside itself a little way, and insert the roll, gradually pushing the end through so that the fabric tube encloses the whole length. Adjust the seam on the fabric tube so that it runs straight along the whole length.

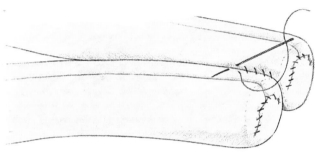

5 Neatening the ends On the unfinished ends, turn in the raw edges neatly, folding them in like the end of a parcel, and slipstitch closed. Position the two long tubes with their seams facing the same way, and catch them together with a few stitches at each end.

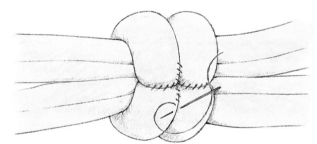

6 Joining the short tubes Wrap a short tube around the middle of the long ones, butting the ends together at the back; hand stitch the ends together neatly. Repeat with the second short tube. Then secure the two tubes together at the back with a few hand stitches.

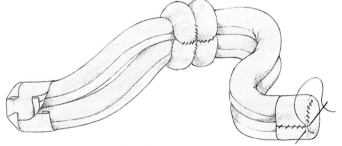

7 Finishing the ends Cut two 23 x 10cm (9 x 4in) pieces of fabric. Press under 1cm (⅜in) on the lower (long) edge and one short side. Right side out, wrap fabric tightly round each end of tieback, folding in the raw edges like a parcel. Slipstitch in place. Using double thread, stitch a curtain ring firmly to each end of the tieback.

The intricately detailed textures of the fabrics used for this double padded tube tieback highlight the cool elegance of a neutral scheme.

Tip

FABRIC LOOPS

If you'd rather hang your tieback on fabric loops, as shown on page 119, cut a 12 x 4cm (4³⁄₄ x 1¹⁄₂in) piece of fabric. Turn in 1cm (³⁄₈in) all round and press. With wrong sides together, fold the strip in half lengthways; stitch all round, close to the edges. Fold double and handsew in place.

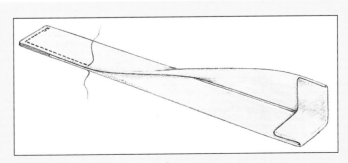

Tube tieback variations

You can use the same basic padded tube to create a variety of interesting tiebacks – you can experiment with different thicknesses of tube, or combine different fabrics to give a decorative touch to a plain and simple window treatment.

Here are three versions to try. You need the same materials as overleaf, depending on the length of tube needed for the tieback. To ring the changes on the double twist tieback, you could make the fabric tube from two contrasting colours.

Jumbo knotted tieback

1 **Making the tube** Following steps **1** and **3-4** on page 120, make up a padded tube one and a half times the desired length plus 102cm (41in).

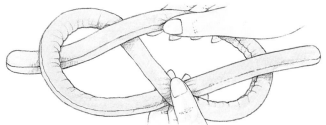

2 **Tying the knot** Bring the tube back on itself in a figure of eight, then push the end through the loop. Push to the centre of the tube and tighten. Trim the inner roll to the desired length; trim the fabric cover, leaving the ends 3cm (1¼in) longer than the inner roll. To finish, turn in and slipstitch ends and stitch a curtain ring on to each end.

Double twist tieback

1 **Making the tube** Following steps **1** and **3-4** on page 120, make up a padded tube four times the desired finished length of tieback.

2 **Twisting the tube** Shut one end securely in a drawer. Holding the other end taut, twist firmly until tube is tightly twisted down its length. Bring two ends together so the tube twists into a skein. Follow step **5** on page 120, and finish by stitching curtains rings on to ends.

Ruched tube tieback

1 **Making the roll and tube** Following step **1** on page 120, make a roll the desired length of the tieback. Following step **3**, make a tube, using a 21cm (8¼in) wide fabric strip, three times the length of the roll.

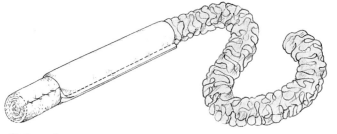

2 **Covering the roll** Follow step **4** on page 120 to cover the roll, easing the extra fabric into even gathers. At the open end of the tube, turn in the raw edges and slipstitch closed, stitching through to the roll inside. Stitch a ring at each end, stitching through to the roll inside.

Exotic baubles

Be bold and go for a different furnishing look with these exotic hanging decorations. Add flair and excitement to a window treatment by suspending them from a valance or letting them dangle from a tieback.

When you are adding the final touch to a window treatment, why just stick to conventional tassels? Dare to be different with these extravagant hanging decorations. Choose an elegant tapered cone, a soft, curvaceous shape, or a combination of both – either way, you will create a strong and unusual interior design statement all your own.

Both accessories require little sewing expertise, and use only small amounts of fabric. Make them from remnants left over from curtains or cushions, or choose other fabrics to echo your colour scheme. Hunt for interesting beads and unusual cords or ropes to complete the effect.

Hang the baubles from a decorative rope as part of a dramatic drapery, or at the end of a pole to draw attention to an attractive finial. You can make smaller versions to trim the corners of a bold table cover, and to add a flourish to simple rope tiebacks.

▲ *These exotic decorations come in two quite different designs – a distinctive cone shape and a series of three graded balls. They are made in rich furnishing fabrics and finished with interesting beads to add a stylish flourish at the end of a decorative rope.*

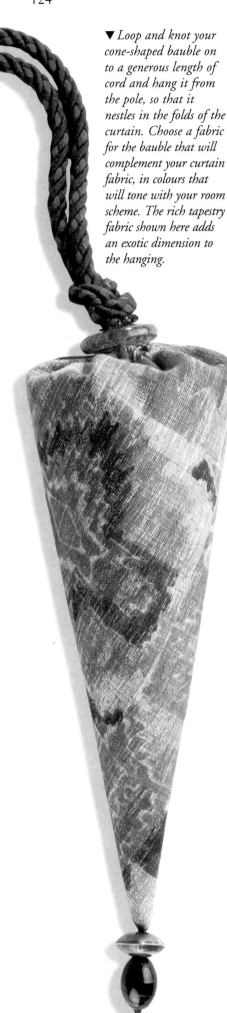

▼ *Loop and knot your cone-shaped bauble on to a generous length of cord and hang it from the pole, so that it nestles in the folds of the curtain. Choose a fabric for the bauble that will complement your curtain fabric, in colours that will tone with your room scheme. The rich tapestry fabric shown here adds an exotic dimension to the hanging.*

Making the cone bauble

The cone-shaped bauble is formed from a quarter-circle cut from stiff buckram or heavyweight non-fusible interfacing. If you have neither of these, use lightweight card instead. The basic cone is covered with fabric, then beads and cord are added for a final flourish.

The instructions given below show how to make a 27cm (10¾in) long cone

bauble, but it can be scaled down by reducing the length of the straight side of the quarter-circle. If you are not sure what would look best in your room, try making up paper cones in a number of different sizes to see which you prefer.

You can use almost any fabric to make the bauble, from firmly woven furnishing cottons to glossy satins and damasks.

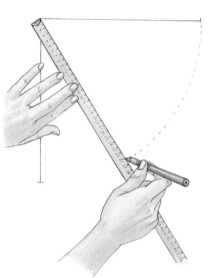

1 Making a quarter-circle pattern
On paper, draw two lines 27cm (10¾in) long at right angles to each other. Then use the ruler to measure and mark a gently curving arc of dots 27cm (10¾in) from the corner. Join up the dots and cut out the quarter-circle shape.

You will need

To make a cone 27cm (10¾in) long:

◆ **43cm (17in) square of furnishing fabric**

◆ **Cord or rope**

◆ **Two large beads and one smaller bead for the base**

◆ **One flat bead for the top**

◆ **30cm (12in) square of buckram or heavyweight interfacing**

◆ **Matching sewing thread**

◆ **Masking tape (optional)**

◆ **Paper, pencil and ruler**

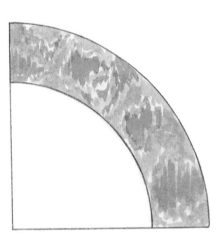

2 Cutting out *From buckram:* use the pattern to cut one quarter circle. *From fabric:* use the pattern to cut one quarter-circle, allowing an extra 14cm (5½in) outside curved edge. To make cone shape, roll buckram into a cone so the straight sides overlap and form a point at the base. Oversew edge to secure shape, or use masking tape.

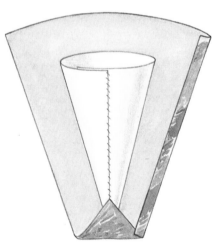

3 Covering the cone with fabric Lay the buckram cone centrally on the wrong side of the fabric. Fold up the point of the fabric over the point of the cone. Then fold 1cm (⅜in) to the wrong side on one straight edge. Roll the fabric tightly round the cone with the folded in edge overlapping the raw edge; slipstitch in place.

You can turn a plain rope tieback into a distinctive accessory by using a single ball or making a scaled-down version of the cone. To use either version, loop the cord round the centre of a plain rope tieback and hang as usual.

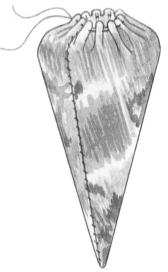

4 Finishing the top Turn in 1cm (⅜in) at the top edge of the fabric. Then work a row of gathering stitches along the top edge, close to the fold. Pull up the gathering thread to close the top of the cone neatly, but do not secure the thread; leave the thread in the needle to finish off later.

5 Adding the beads Secure a thread to the point of the cone with a couple of tiny stitches. Pass the needle through both large beads, then through the smaller bead. Pass the thread back up through the large beads again and fasten it off securely with a few more tiny stitches at the base of the cone.

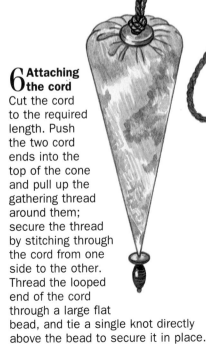

6 Attaching the cord Cut the cord to the required length. Push the two cord ends into the top of the cone and pull up the gathering thread around them; secure the thread by stitching through the cord from one side to the other. Thread the looped end of the cord through a large flat bead, and tie a single knot directly above the bead to secure it in place.

Making the round decoration

Three soft balls in graduating sizes make up this decoration. They are stuffed with polyester toy filling so they hold their shape, and are joined together with beads and cord.

The instructions given here are for a decoration approximately 24cm (9½in) long. You can make a smaller decoration by reducing the size of the balls, or use just one large ball, decorated with beads, for a different look.

Soft lustrous velvet in rich jewel colours would be an exotic alternative to printed cotton furnishing fabrics. Instead of beads, you could use a silky tassel in a toning or matching colour.

You will need

To make a decoration 24cm (9½in) long:

- ◆ Furnishing fabric
- ◆ Two large beads and one smaller bead
- ◆ Matching sewing thread
- ◆ Polyester toy filling
- ◆ Long needle, button thread
- ◆ Cord or rope

1 Cutting out the shapes *From the fabric:* cut three rectangles to the following measurements: 38 x 18cm (15 x 7in); 30 x 14cm (12 x 5½in); and 25 x 11cm (10 x 4¼in).

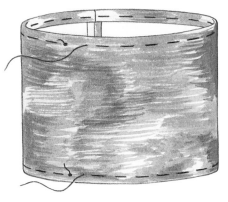

2 Making the large ball With right sides together and taking a 1cm (⅜in) seam allowance, stitch the short ends of the largest rectangle together. Fold 1cm (⅜in) to the wrong side at the top and bottom edges. Work a row of gathering stitches close to the top and bottom folds.

3 Finishing the ball Pull up the bottom row of gathering stitches tightly and secure with a few stitches. Fill the ball with polyester toy filling to make a soft, rounded shape. Pull up the top row of gathering stitches tightly and secure as before.

4 Making the other balls Repeat steps 2-3 using the two smaller rectangles of fabric.

5 Joining balls Using a long needle, secure a length of button thread to the top of the largest ball. Pass the needle through all three balls in the order shown, emerging at the bottom of the smallest ball. Next, thread the needle through two large beads, then through the smaller bead. Pass the needle back up through the large beads and through the balls, emerging back at the top of the largest ball. Secure the thread with a few stitches.

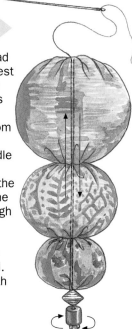

6 Attaching the cord Cut and attach the cord to the top of the largest ball, following *Making the cone bauble*, step **6**.

Index

Picture Acknowledgements

Photographs: 7 Robert Harding Syndication/Homes and Gardens/Debi Treloar, 8(t) Eaglemoss/Paul Bricknell, (bl) Robert Harding Syndication/Homes and Interiors/Russell Sadur, (br) Eaglemoss/Adrian Taylor, 9(t) Harlequin Fabrics, (bru) Eaglemoss/Adrian Taylor, (br) Robert Harding Syndication/Homes and Gardens/Jan Baldwin, 10(t) Robert Harding Syndication/Homes and Gardens/Trevor Richards, (bl) Eaglemoss/Paul Bricknell, (br) Elizabeth Whiting and Associates/Brian Harrison, 11 Robert Harding Syndication/IPC Magazines/Ideal Home, 12(tl) Eaglemoss/Tif Hunter, (tr) Eaglemoss/Graham Rae, (b) Eaglemoss/Sue Atkinson, 13 Eaglemoss/Graham Rae, 14 Eaglemoss/Sue Atkinson, 15 Arthur Sanderson and Sons, 16 Laura Ashley, 17 Next Interiors, 19(t) Robert Harding Syndication/IPC Magazines/Ideal Home, (b) Next Interiors, 20 Laura Ashley, 21 Filigree Stiebel, 22 Eaglemoss/Paul Bricknell, 23 Robert Harding Syndication/IPC Magazines/Homes and Gardens, 24(t) Laura Ashley, (l) Eaglemoss/Paul Bricknell, (b) Eaglemoss/Steve Tanner, 25,26 Robert Harding Syndication/IPC Magazines, 27 Eaglemoss/Paul Bricknell, 28 Robert Harding Syndication/IPC Magazines, 29 Robert Harding Syndication/Homes and Gardens/Country Homes and Interiors, 31 rhs/IPC Magazines/David Chivers, 32 Robert Harding Syndication/Homes and Gardens/Trevor Richards, 33,34 Robert Harding Syndication/IPC Magazines/Ideal Home, 35 Harlequin Fabrics, 36 Eaglemoss/Adrian Taylor, 37 Biggie Best, 39, 40 Eaglemoss/Lizzie Orme, 41 Robert Harding Syndication/IPC Magazines/Country Homes and Interiors, 42 Harlequin, 43 Warner Fabrics, 44 Robert Harding Syndication/IPC Magazines/Homes and Gardens, 45-47 Rufflette, 48 Eaglemoss/Lizzie Orme, 49 Crowson Fabrics, 50 Forbo-Lancaster, 51 Robert Harding Syndication/Homes and Gardens/Polly Wreford, 53 Harrison Drapes, 54 Harlequin, 55 Harrison Drapes, 57 Robert Harding Syndication/Homes and Interiors/Dominic Blackmore, 58 Robert Harding Syndication/Homes and Gardens/H.Bourg, 59 Robert Harding Syndication/IPC Magazines/Homes and Interiors, 61 Robert Harding Syndication/IPC Magazines/Homes and Gardens, 62 Integra Products, 63 Robert Harding Syndication/Country Homes and Interiors/Andreas von Einsiedel, 65 Elizabeth Whiting and Associates/Andreas von Einsiedel, 66 Robert Harding Syndication/Homes and Gardens/Trevor Richards, 67 Elizabeth Whiting and Associates/James Merrel, 69 Harris Fabrics, Dorato Collection, 70 Harrison Drape, 71 Osborne and Little, 73 Coloroll, 74 Eaglemoss/Lizzie Orme, 77 Robert Harding Syndication/IPC Magazines/Country Homes and Interiors, 79 Romo Fabrics, 80 Robert Harding Syndication/IPC Magazines/Country Homes and Interiors, 81 Robert Harding Syndication/Country Homes and Interiors/Christopher Drake, 83 Biggie Best, 84 Robert Harding Syndication/IPC Magazines/Country Homes and Interiors, 85 Robert Harding Syndication/Homes and Gardens/Christopher Drake, 87 Ariadne, Holland, 88 Robert Harding Syndication/Homes and Interiors Dominic Blackmore, 89 Robert Harding Syndication/Country Homes and Interiors/Christopher Drake, 90(t) Elizabeth Whiting and Associates/Rodney Hyett, (b) Robert Harding Syndication/Homes and Gardens/James Merrel, 91(t) Robert Harding Syndication/Homes and Gardens/Trevor Richards, (bl) Robert Harding Syndication/Homes and Gardens/Debi Treloar, (br) Eaglemoss/Lizzie Orme, 92(t) Robert Harding Syndication/Homes and Gardens/Andreas von Einsiedel, (bl) Harlequin, (br) Eaglemoss/Graham Rae, 93-95 Baby & Peuter, Holland, 97 Eaglemoss/Graham Rae, 99 Elizabeth Whiting and Associates, 100 David Parmiter, 101 Robert Harding Syndication/Country Homes and Interiors/Tim Imrie, 102 Robert Harding Syndication/Homes and Interiors/Dominic Blackmore, 103 Margriet, Holland, 105-106 Ariadne, Holland, 107, 109 Eaglemoss/Simon Page-Ritchie, 110 Arthur Sanderson and Sons, 111 Eaglemoss/Graham Rae, 113 Eaglemoss/Martin Chaffer, 114 Eaglemoss, 115-118 Eaglemoss/Graham Rae, 119 Biggie Best, 121 Eaglemoss/Lizzie Orme, 122 Cy deCosse, 123(t) Eaglemoss/Lizzie Orme, (br) Eaglemoss/Paul Bricknell, 124 Eaglemoss/Lizzie Orme.

Illustrations: 75-75 Kuo Kang Chen. All others John Hutchinson.